BORN WITHOUT PERMISSION

EMBRACING THE UNSEEN STRENGTH TO BREAK FREE

A CELESTIN IGNATIUS RAJ

To my father,

A Celestin Ignatius Raj—

The man who gave me a name that once made me question myself, and later gave me the courage to define it. You taught me that a name gains power not from how it's pronounced, but from how it's lived. Thank you for planting the fire, for raising a son who would learn to carry his storm with dignity. This book is not just written by me—it is written through the strength you quietly passed on.

Contents

Preface

There are books that begin as ideas.

And then there are books like this—Born Without Permission—that begin as a war within.

I never intended to write this. Not as a book. Not in words. I was just trying to make sense of the world that kept handing me labels I never asked for—too different, too ambitious, too unrealistic, too much. At times, I believed them. Other times, I broke beneath them. But eventually, I chose to break them instead.

This book is a rebellion, not in anger—but in honesty. It's about the quiet, burning fire that lives inside those who were told to fit in but were born to break out. It's about the bumblebee that flies anyway, the child who speaks on stage despite fear, the failure that teaches louder than success, the name that becomes a legacy, and the voice that fights through the noise.

Born Without Permission is for anyone who has ever doubted themselves because the world gave them a mirror filled with lies. If you've ever stood in a room and felt like you didn't belong, or if you've ever stayed up wondering if your dreams are too loud for the life you're living—this book is for you.

I don't offer you a roadmap. I offer you stories—real, raw, messy, and mine. I offer you truths I had to bleed for. And I offer you the one thing I wish someone gave me when I was young and lost:

Permission to be exactly who you are.

If you're willing to walk into the fire, I'll walk with you. Not as a teacher, but as a fellow traveler who finally chose to believe.

— Celestin Ignatius Raj

Epigraph

"வரெ-வந்த- வலெஃகிய ஆக்கம் அத-வல்ல கர-வி கடைபீட- இலான்." - திர-க்க-றள் **596**

Meaning: "Wealth gained through fear or flattery is not true wealth; real achievement comes from one who never compromises on self-respect or courage."

Introduction Born Without Permission

This book isn't here to hand you a magic formula or feed you the usual "Be brave" or "Just be confident" lines — no, that's not what this is about. This book is a wake-up call. Because somewhere along the way, we all forgot something simple, raw, and real: that we were all born with the same basic tools — eyes to see, a mind to think, a voice to speak, and a heart to feel. Yet somehow, we've convinced ourselves that we're not enough. That we have to tweak, shrink, or reshape who we are just to be accepted. That we need to fit in to be seen as worthy. Let me give you a simple example: you put on a shirt you love — your vibe, your choice — and you feel good in it, confident. But someone says, "It doesn't suit you." Maybe they're trying to help, maybe not. You brush it off. But then another person says the same thing. And another. Suddenly, that shirt you once loved becomes the shirt you'll never wear again. Not because the shirt changed, but because something inside you did. Their opinions didn't steal the fabric — they stole your joy. They chipped away at your confidence. And that's what we do, every day — we trade little pieces of ourselves for approval. We let the noise become the truth. We let the outside voices drown out the one that matters most: our own. And in that quiet, we forget how to be free. But that moment — when you feel that crack, that sting, that shift — that's your awakening. That's the moment you stop handing over your happiness like it's up for debate. That's the moment you remember that you're the king of your mind — just an organ sitting up there, wrapped in bone and flesh, yet I treat mine like a throne. A throne filled with untold stories, bold truths, and unshakable thoughts — not a sponge soaking in everyone else's opinions. They told me to wait my turn. To play it safe. Stay quiet. Be normal. Blend in. But I was never made for smallness. I wasn't born to follow rules written for someone else's comfort. I was born without permission. And this book? It's not about being fearless. It's about being real — in a world drowning in filters, noise, and fakery. It's about building a spine so solid that no rejection, no failure, no opinion can shake you. You don't need validation. You don't need a spotlight. You don't even need to have everything figured out. You just need one thing: you. Fully. Unapologetically. You. The version of you that stopped asking for permission, and started taking the damn shot.

I

The Lie We're Told

when I was young, they told me, "You need to fit in to succeed." Sound familiar? That's the first lie most of us are handed, disguised as wisdom, wrapped in fear, and passed down like tradition. We're taught to walk a certain way, talk a certain way, be agreeable, speak only when spoken to, and never make too much noise. Blend in. Be polite. Be safe. Be average. And maybe, just maybe... you'll be accepted. But here's what no one tells you: the world was never changed by someone who played it safe. From the very first day of school, we're pushed to stay within the lines. Don't draw outside the box. Don't question the rules. Don't love too loudly. Don't dream too big. If you show passion, they'll tell you to be "practical." If you think differently, they'll try to fix you. I learned that the hard way. I was nine years old. My dad would drop me off at a public swimming pool every morning. It was massive, a place where grown men and women in their 30s and 40s swam laps with grace and power. I was the only child among them. And like every kid, I was instructed to stay in the shallow end — four feet of water, just enough to keep me safe. "You're too young," they said. "It's dangerous." And maybe they were right, because one day, I slipped. I ventured too far. I panicked. I went under. I drowned — not completely, but enough to taste what helplessness feels like. Someone pulled me out, and I coughed and cried and sat by the pool's edge in silence. That moment etched itself into my mind. And for a while, I stopped asking. Stopped trying. Stopped dreaming about the deep end. Fear has a funny way of disguising itself as wisdom. But deep down, a quiet fire still burned in me. I trained harder. I watched. I learned. I refused to let one moment define the rest of my life. I rebuilt my confidence, stroke by stroke, breath by breath. Weeks passed. And then one day, I asked again. The lifeguards hesitated, but they saw something in me. Something unshakable. They gave me a nod. I stepped to the edge, took a breath, and dove into twenty feet of water. I didn't drown. I didn't panic. I swam like I had always belonged there. When I reached the other side, I pulled myself up and turned to see their faces. Not angry. Not surprised. Just silent and stunned. In that moment, everything shifted. Not just how they saw me, but how I saw myself. That day wasn't about swimming. It was about reclaiming my power. It was about proving, to them and to myself, that I didn't need permission to rise. That just because I fell once didn't mean I was meant to stay down. And just because I was told to stay in the shallow end didn't mean I belonged there.

The Shark in the Tank

There's a story I once read that hit me like a punch to the soul. The story of the shark in the tank. A marine biologist placed a shark into a large aquarium and introduced a few small bait fish. As expected, the shark lunged forward and devoured them instantly. Then, she installed a thick sheet of fiberglass across the center of the tank, separating the shark from a fresh batch of fish. The shark charged again, only this time, it slammed hard into the invisible wall. Confused, it tried again. And again. And again. Every time, it failed. Days passed. The shark grew tired. The once-ferocious predator began hitting the divider with less intensity, then only occasionally, until one day, it stopped trying altogether. It floated in its half of the tank, conditioned to believe the barrier was permanent. That's when the scientist removed the divider entirely. Now, the tank was open. No walls. No barriers. Just water and fish.

Freedom. But the shark didn't move. It had been trained by failure. It had been broken by belief. Even when the path was clear, it stayed put, trapped not by the glass, but by its own mind. That shark? That's all of us at some point. We've all been told we can't do something. We've all been laughed at, doubted, dismissed. And each time we hit that invisible wall — a rejection, a failure, a fear — we lose a little bit of our fight. Until one day, we stop chasing what we once wanted. Not because it's out of reach, but because we've convinced ourselves it is. We stop raising our hands. We stop stepping forward. We stop diving in. Not because we're weak, but because we've been taught to doubt our own strength. But here's the truth no one screams loudly enough: those walls were never real. They were just someone else's fears, passed down to us. The fiberglass was never permanent, and neither is your self-doubt. So ask yourself, what's the invisible wall in your life? Is it something someone once said? A failure you haven't forgiven yourself for? A voice in your head that says "you're not ready yet"? Whatever it is, it's not your reality, unless you let it be. You weren't born to swim in circles. You weren't born to settle. And you sure as hell weren't born to stay in the shallow end. If the world tells you to sit down, stand taller. If they say you're too young, too bold, too much — be more. Dive in. Even if you've drowned once. Especially if you have. Because true greatness begins the moment you stop believing in the wall and start believing in yourself.

The Ignatius Theory of Internal Fire

Core Premise:*Confidence and courage are not inherited traits — they are sparked from a deep inner fire that ignites when purpose, discomfort, and self-dialogue align.*

Introduction: The Myth of Natural Confidence

We often admire the bold. The fearless. The speaker who commands a stage, the leader who walks into the unknown, the dreamer who dares to act. We assume they were born with something we lack — a natural confidence coded into their DNA.

But what if that assumption is false? What if courage isn't born, but built?

The Ignatius Theory of Internal Fire is a science-rooted, soul-driven framework that dismantles the myth of inherited bravery. It asserts that confidence is not a personality trait but a mental process — one that can be consciously activated, trained, and sculpted. Like a fire, it starts with a spark: a reason to act. It grows with friction, heat, and pressure. And it's sustained by the oxygen of your inner dialogue.

This chapter introduces a three-pillar model to ignite that fire within — a formula that can transform doubt into daring.

Pillar 1: Purpose Activation (The 'Why' Catalyst)

"Purpose is the flint that sparks the flame of courage."

Confidence isn't just the belief in yourself — it's the belief in the reason you must act. When your actions are tethered to a meaningful "why," hesitation becomes irrelevant.

The brain's decision-making system isn't powered by logic alone; it's deeply emotional. Neuroscientific research reveals that the **ventromedial prefrontal cortex (vmPFC)** is activated when we make decisions aligned with our values. This part of the brain quiets fear and amplifies conviction when our choices align with purpose. When you believe that your action matters — that someone, somewhere needs what you're about to do — fear loses its grip. This is not motivational fluff. It's biology.

Example: The Reluctant Orator

A shy student, terrified of public speaking, volunteers to give a speech. Not because he wants applause, but because he believes someone in the room needs to hear his story. The purpose is bigger than the fear. And that makes all the difference.

Key Takeaways:

- Clarity of purpose overrides fear responses.
- Purpose fuels persistence; without it, courage burns out quickly.
- Aligning actions with values engages the brain's courage circuitry.

Pillar 2: Discomfort Conditioning (The Bravery Gym)

"Fear is not the enemy. It's the gym where courage is built."

We tend to avoid discomfort. But what if discomfort was the very ingredient needed to build courage? Like muscles in a weight room, bravery strengthens with resistance.

When you willingly choose discomfort — by taking small, fear-inducing actions repeatedly — you rewire your brain's fear response system. The **amygdala**, our internal alarm system, becomes less reactive over time through exposure. This is not just a psychological theory; it's a documented result of **exposure therapy and neuroplasticity.**

This practice of "bravery reps" is like lifting heavier weights each day. The more you do it, the stronger you become. Not because fear disappears, but because your tolerance grows.

Example: Rejection Training

An introvert sends 100 cold emails — something that once paralyzed him. At email #5, he shakes. At email #50, he's unbothered. By email #100, rejection has no sting. Fear is now familiar — and therefore powerless.

Discomfort Is a Teacher:

- It teaches that fear is survivable.
- It builds "bravery circuits" that strengthen with repetition.
- It shifts your identity from "avoider" to "approacher."

Pillar 3: Internal Dialogue Sculpting (The Voice That Builds You)

"You are the voice you listen to the most."

The way you speak to yourself — in moments of doubt, in silence, in stress — shapes your confidence more than any external validation ever could.

Neuroscience confirms that **positive self-talk** activates the **anterior cingulate cortex and insula** — regions associated with emotional regulation, motivation, and reduced anxiety. Simply put, your internal narrative can calm your nervous system or amplify your panic.

The Ignatius Theory proposes a powerful idea: you are not born with *a self-image; you speak it into existence.* When your inner voice evolves from critic to coach, your entire identity follows.

Example: Narrative Reframing

"I can't do this" becomes "I've done harder things." That one narrative shift changes posture, focus, and action. Identity is rewritten, not with affirmations, but with evidence-based reminders of resilience.

How to Sculpt Your Inner Voice:

- Track your most common negative thoughts and rewrite them.
- Speak to yourself as you would a friend you believe in.
- Turn doubt into data: "What does this fear say about what I care about?"

The Formula of Internal Fire

Let's now bring it all together into one elegant, actionable equation:

Confidence = (Purpose × Discomfort) + Self-Talk

Each component compounds the other:

- Purpose gives you a reason to act despite fear.
- Discomfort builds familiarity with fear and stretches your courage.
- Self-talk locks in the identity of someone who acts boldly.

This is not magic. It's mechanics. With this formula, confidence is no longer a mystery or a gift. It's a system anyone can train.

Scientific Backbone

The Ignatius Theory isn't just intuitive — it's scientific. It draws from:

- **Bandura's Self-Efficacy Theory:** We act when we believe we can influence outcomes.

- **Neuroplasticity Research:** Repeated experiences (like discomfort or self-talk) reshape the brain.
- **Exposure Therapy:** Gradual exposure to fears lowers emotional reactivity.
- **Cognitive Behavioral Science:** Thoughts shape behavior and emotional outcomes.

Why This Theory Matters

The Ignatius Theory offers a rare combination of:

- **Simplicity:** A memorable, actionable framework.
- **Scientific Integrity:** Grounded in verified neuroscience and psychology.
- **Accessibility:** Applicable to anyone, from a teenager facing exams to a CEO navigating crises.
- **Depth:** It doesn't bypass fear — it transforms it.

Most importantly, this theory is **authentic.** It was born not in a lab, but in lived experience. From that trembling moment before a school speech about photosynthesis to today, where words have become a calling, this journey validates the theory: Confidence is built. And anyone can build it.

Final Word: Lighting Your Fire

You don't have to wait for confidence to arrive before you act. You can create it. You can spark your internal fire with a powerful purpose, stoke it through deliberate discomfort, and protect it with the warmth of your own voice.

(The Ignatius Theory isn't just a path. It's a torch. Carry it. Pass it on.)

The Flame of Your Own Confidence

It's easy to get lost in the noise of the world. The world that tells you that you're not enough. That you need to wait, be perfect, be ready. That the confident ones are the lucky ones. But what if that's not true? What if the confidence you seek is not something to be discovered, but something to be made — by you, through every step you take, every discomfort you face, and every word you tell yourself?

The Ignatius Theory isn't some abstract concept — it's a blueprint. A blueprint that is rooted in the science of how the brain works, how we act, and how we evolve. It's a simple, actionable method that you can follow to create your own internal fire — to build a confidence that's unshakable.

And here's the secret: You don't have to wait for the perfect moment. You don't have to wait for the world to tell you you're ready. You start now. You start with your purpose. You start with choosing discomfort. You start by changing the way you speak to yourself.

The biggest breakthroughs don't come from waiting in the shadows. They come from stepping into the light — even when it's blinding. Even when it's scary. And yes, even when you've failed before. The fire inside you doesn't grow by avoiding fear; it grows by facing it.

Think back to the shark in the tank. The moment the shark stopped trying to break through the glass, it wasn't because the glass was unbreakable. It was because the shark had been conditioned to believe it couldn't. That's what the world does to us — it convinces us that our limits are permanent. It tells us that we've failed once, so we can never try again. But just like that shark, the moment you realize that those walls were never real, you start moving again. You start swimming again.

And that's where true power lies — not in never failing, but in knowing that failure doesn't define you. The moments when you feel lost, when you feel like you're drowning in doubt, are the very moments that define your strength. These are the moments that will determine whether you stay in the shallow end or dive into the deep, whether you live within someone else's limits or create your own.

I know that it's hard. The road to building confidence isn't easy. It requires a commitment to your own growth. It requires you to dive into the discomfort, to push past the moments of fear and doubt, and to tell yourself, "I am enough." It requires you to constantly remind yourself that you are not your failures. You are not your fears. You are not the walls others built around you. You are the fire that will burn through them.

When you ignite your purpose, when you learn to embrace discomfort as the gym for your courage, and when you rewrite your internal narrative to reflect your power — that's when everything changes. Not just for you, but for everyone around you. Because as you rise, as you build your fire, you become a beacon for others to do the same. Your confidence doesn't just light up your world; it illuminates the path for others to follow.

So, stop waiting for permission. You don't need it. The only approval you need is your own. And it's time to start believing in the fire within you — the fire that has always been there, waiting for you to recognize it, waiting for you to fuel it.

It's not about being fearless. It's about finding your purpose, stepping into the discomfort, and speaking to yourself like someone you truly believe in. When you do that, confidence won't just show up one day. It will already be there, glowing inside you, lighting your way forward.

Your internal fire is ready to burn brighter than any doubt. **Will you light it?**

II

The Bumblebee Principle

The Myth That Set Us Free

Have you ever heard that curious story about bumblebees, the one that science once claimed was true? According to the laws of aerodynamics, bumblebees should not be able to fly. It's often cited as one of the most perplexing and counterintuitive facts in nature. Why? Well, if you look at the proportions of a bumblebee's body and wings—its massive body and relatively small wings—conventional physics suggests that its flight shouldn't be possible. Their wings are too small and their bodies too large, defying the principles of aerodynamics. For years, scientists would argue that, based on their size and shape, bumblebees simply shouldn't have the ability to lift off the ground.

Yet, despite all of these scientific calculations, bumblebees have been flying for millions of years. They dart and hover through gardens, around flowers, over fields, effortlessly taking off into the sky. They are fully unaware of the fact that science says they shouldn't be able to fly. They don't hesitate or question their own abilities. They simply take flight.

In many ways, this is a metaphor for how we live our lives. The bumblebee's flight doesn't rely on understanding why it's possible; it just knows that it can. Imagine if we all approached our lives with the same mindset. How often do we allow ourselves to be limited by external definitions of what is possible or impossible? We're constantly told by society, by well-meaning family and friends, and by our own fears and doubts, that certain things are just beyond us. We internalize these limitations, folding our wings and never attempting to take flight. We let the doubts, rules, and boundaries of the world around us dictate what we can or cannot do.

But here's the profound truth that the bumblebee reminds us of: the world's logic and external limitations don't have to define your potential. The only thing that defines your limits is whether or not you decide to push beyond them. The bumblebee isn't concerned with the fact that scientists say it shouldn't be able to fly. It doesn't have the self-awareness to question its capabilities—it just does what it was made to do. It takes off, flaps its wings, and soars.

The Limitations We Place On Ourselves

How often do we let the opinions of others limit what we believe is possible for ourselves? In the same way the world told the bumblebee it couldn't fly, we are often told—either overtly or subtly—that our dreams are out of reach. Society tells us what's normal, what's safe, and what's "realistic." We're conditioned to follow a certain path, to fit into predefined boxes, and to strive for conventional success. We're told to play by the rules, to do what others have done before us, and to expect things to happen in a linear way.

But what if the rules don't apply to you? What if, just like the bumblebee, you can fly because you refuse to accept the limits that others have placed upon you? What if the only thing standing between you and your dreams is your willingness to try, to flap your wings, and to take action despite the noise of doubt?

When we begin to question the limitations set upon us—by society, by our families, or even by our own fears—we unlock a powerful form of freedom. The freedom to redefine success on our own terms. The freedom to pursue what sets our souls on fire, not what others deem worthy of pursuit. The world may say you can't fly, but if you don't question that belief and take action, you'll never know if you can.

Living with Purpose, Not Limitation

Imagine, for a moment, that you could live with the same freedom the bumblebee has. Picture a life where you are blissfully unaware of the constraints others have placed on your potential. How different would you approach your dreams? What would you do if you didn't doubt your ability to succeed or fear failure? What if you stopped asking for permission to pursue what you love?

When you stop worrying about the impossibility of your dreams and focus solely on your "why"—your purpose—the sky's the limit.

The bumblebee doesn't question the physics of flight. It doesn't waste time wondering if it's good enough or deserving enough to fly. It simply flies. And this is where we need to draw the parallel: we too must let go of the need to fit into a box, to follow the prescribed path. Instead, we should focus on our purpose—the reason why we want to fly in the first place. When we align with that purpose, our confidence takes off, just like the bumblebee.

The Freedom of Belief: Breaking Through Self-Imposed Boundaries

What makes the bumblebee's flight so special isn't just that it flies in the face of convention—it's that it flies without self-doubt. The bumblebee doesn't waste time thinking, "I'm too big to fly" or "My wings are too small." It doesn't question its right to soar. It just flies because that's what it's meant to do.

And this is where we often trip ourselves up. We question our worthiness, our ability, and our right to pursue what feels impossible. But what if we could take a page from the bumblebee's book and believe, without hesitation, that we too can soar—no matter what the world tells us?

What's holding you back? Is it fear? Doubt? Or the voices that say you're not good enough? These are the same barriers that society places in front of you. And just like the bumblebee, you can choose to break through them. The only thing standing between you and your dreams is the courage to try.

Taking Flight: What Will Your "Flight" Look Like?

It's time to stop waiting for the "perfect moment" or the "perfect conditions." The bumblebee doesn't wait for the winds to align or for the perfect moment to fly—it simply takes off. And so should you.

Ask yourself: What would your life look like if you decided to take action right now? What could you achieve if you stopped hesitating and trusted in your own potential?

What if you simply believed in your ability to soar, just like the bumblebee does, without asking for permission from anyone? You may not know all the answers or have everything figured out.

But that's part of the beauty of it. The flight isn't about perfection—it's about courage, purpose, and the willingness to trust yourself.

The Day I Took the Mic

Let me take you back to a day that should have been like any other. I was just a regular fifth grader, quietly sitting in a classroom where the louder, more confident voices always seemed to dominate the space. Public speaking? That was something for the outgoing kids, the ones who thrived under the spotlight. But then, something unexpected happened.

Our teacher asked if anyone wanted to give a short speech during the assembly. I remember the room growing still for a second, as everyone avoided eye contact, hoping someone else would volunteer. But before I could stop myself, my hand shot up. I still don't know why it happened. I wasn't the confident type. I hated attention. And yet, here I was, volunteering for something that terrified me.

That was the beginning. My name appeared on the board, and the gravity of the moment hit me all at once. My mind went blank. I rushed home that day, nervously practicing my speech in front of a cracked mirror. Words like "photosynthesis" seemed like mountains, and every time I repeated them, my tongue felt like it was betraying me. My voice quivered with every sentence. I imagined freezing in front of the entire school.

Then the day arrived. The assembly hall was crowded, and there I stood at the front, clutching my paper like it was my only lifeline. The microphone seemed to loom larger than ever. The silence around me felt thick, like it was pressing in on me, suffocating me. My hands shook. And at that moment, I almost wanted to turn around and run. But then something happened. I saw my teacher at the back of the room. She gave me a subtle nod, a silent assurance that I was okay—that I could do this.

With that small gesture, I found the courage to speak. At first, my words stumbled out, slow and shaky. But as I continued, I found a rhythm. The more I spoke, the stronger my voice became. By the end of my speech, I wasn't just reading the words—I was saying them, believing in them. The applause at the end felt like a distant echo, because the true victory wasn't in the approval of others—it was in the realization that I could do something I never thought I could.

That day wasn't about delivering the perfect speech. Far from it. I wasn't the best. But that's when I learned the most valuable lesson of all: you don't have to be perfect to succeed. You just have to try. I gave myself permission to be brave. And that moment, simple as it seemed, set something alight within me.

Beneath His Shadow

If you ever wonder about the power of perseverance, let me tell you a story that completely changed my perspective. It's about my father—who, by all accounts, should have given up long before he found his way.

He grew up in the heart of Bangalore, attending a small Kannada-medium school. Life there was straightforward. It was a place where everyone spoke the same language, shared the same customs, and followed a rhythm that felt natural. But then everything changed. He was admitted to an elite English-medium school, a place where the world was turned upside down. It was called Lords Boys School, and to my father, it felt like an alien world.

The transition was brutal. Suddenly, all the books were in English, a language he barely knew. The assignments were foreign, the teachers strict, especially Miss Kamala Gowda—one of the hardest, no-nonsense disciplinarians you could imagine. He felt completely out of place. The other boys seemed to breeze through, while he struggled just to keep up. His homework was filled with mistakes, his test papers marked in angry red ink. Each day, he walked into that classroom with a sense of dread.

He could have given up. He could have told himself that he didn't belong in a school like that, that he was simply too far behind. And in a way, everyone around him probably expected him to. But there was something in him—a spark, a fire—that refused to accept that story.

One evening, after another scolding from Miss Kamala, he made a vow to himself. "This ends now," he said, his voice steady with resolve. "I won't let this define me." That was the turning point. It was in that moment of frustration and pain that he found his true power.

From then on, my father set a new course for himself. He practiced English every single day—sometimes reciting newspaper articles, sometimes copying pages from textbooks just to familiarize himself with the language. He would ask questions even when he felt embarrassed. Every mistake was a lesson. Every failure became fuel for his determination.

The transformation didn't happen overnight. But over time, he started improving. Slowly, his confidence grew. His grades rose. He stopped fearing his teachers and started earning their respect. Eventually, Miss Kamala herself noticed the change. She stopped scolding him, and even made him the class monitor.

Years later, when we visited her, my father proudly said, "This is the teacher who changed my life." She smiled, shaking her head. "Dai rascal... I knew you had it in you," she said with a laugh, proud of the man he had become.

But that story isn't just about academics or climbing to the top of the class. It's about something much more profound. It's about reclaiming your narrative—refusing to let the world define who you are or what you're capable of. My father's story taught me that where you start doesn't determine where you end up. You may face setbacks. You may struggle. But your story is yours to write, no matter the odds. His journey wasn't just a triumph of intelligence—it was a triumph of the heart, a testament to the fire within that refuses to be extinguished. That lesson has burned in me ever since. It's the same fire that pushed me to take the mic in front of my classmates. It's the same fire that refuses to let failure define us. It's the fire that drives us to rise, even when everything around us seems impossible.

Turning Doubt into Determination

Doubt is something we all face, an ever-present shadow that looms over our efforts, dreams, and ambitions. It's a constant companion, whispering in our ears, telling us that we're not ready, that we're not enough, that we should wait for the "perfect moment." But here's the secret: doubt is never going to vanish completely. The question is—will you let it paralyze you, or will you move through it?

The most successful people don't wait for doubt to disappear. They don't sit around hoping for clarity or confidence to magically appear. Instead, they move through the doubt. They take action even when they're scared. They feel the fear and take the next step anyway. They hear the criticism and create despite it. Why? Because they understand a simple, yet powerful truth: the voice that says, "You're not ready," will always be there, but it's not in charge. They are.

Every time we doubt ourselves, we strengthen the story we tell ourselves: that we're not good enough, not capable enough, not ready for what's ahead. But here's the reality—this story is a lie. A lie that we've been telling ourselves for far too long. You were born with everything you need to become who you're meant to be. Every dream you have, every vision of success you hold, is rooted in the truth that you already possess what it takes. You don't need external validation to begin. You don't need certainty to act. You simply need to start.

Think about a baby learning to walk. It doesn't stop to calculate the risks of falling. It doesn't say, "I'll wait until I'm sure I won't stumble." No, it just stands up. It wobbles. It falls. And then it gets up again. And again. And again. It learns to walk not by waiting for perfection, but by embracing the mess, the uncertainty, and the inevitable falls along the way.

We, too, learn by moving. We build confidence through discomfort. Through failure. Through those small, sometimes painful steps that seem to lead nowhere—only to discover that they were, in fact, leading us exactly where we needed to go. The truth is, confidence isn't something you're given. It's something you build, moment by moment, through action, even in the face of uncertainty.

So, the next time doubt rears its head and whispers that you're not enough, remember this: the doubt isn't the problem. The real problem is when we let that doubt define us. Keep moving. Keep trying. Keep growing. Because every step you take, even if it's small, is one step closer to your true potential.

What If You Gave Yourself Permission?

Most of us live life like we're waiting in a queue—for permission, for clarity, for the right time. But what if you stopped waiting?

What if, instead of seeking approval, you decided to approve yourself? To back yourself? To believe that you're allowed to want big things, dream wild dreams, and take bold steps—even if the world isn't clapping for you yet?

Permission Slip Activity

Write this down. Right now. In your own handwriting. Say it out loud. Own it.

Permission Slip

Today, I give myself permission to believe I am enough. To stop hiding. To stop shrinking. To stop waiting for someone to tell me I'm ready.

Today, I give myself permission to dream boldly, act bravely, and fail forward.

I give myself permission to take up space. To speak up. To show up. To rise.

Because I don't need wings that make sense to others.

I just need to fly.

Hang this somewhere. Carry it in your journal. When doubt visits—and it will—read it again.

※

Dare to Fly Anyway

No one was born confident. No one becomes fearless. The only difference between those who rise and those who remain stuck is this: the courage to act despite fear.

You don't need the perfect plan. You don't need all the answers. You just need to begin. Even when your wings feel too small. Even when your dreams feel too heavy. Even when the voices around you whisper that you can't.

Let them talk.

Be the bumblebee. Fly anyway.

III

The Fire Doesn't Wait for Permission

No one sends you an invitation to be yourself. No golden letter arrives with a wax seal that says, "Now, you may finally belong." No divine applause booms from the sky when you decide to rise. And still—against the noise, the doubts, the silence—you rise. That's the secret no one tells you: you're already enough the moment you decide to be.

I was born into a world that didn't know what to make of me. A world obsessed with categories, measurements, and the approval of others. From the moment we're old enough to speak, we're taught to ask for permission: to sit, to speak, to dream. We're handed invisible scripts that tell us who we can be, how far we're allowed to go, and what dreams are "realistic." But I've come to understand something—something I hope you don't just read, but feel: if you keep waiting for someone to say you're worthy, you'll wait your entire life.

I've been an outsider. The kid who spoke differently, looked differently, thought differently. I've walked into rooms where I could feel the silent question floating above me like smog: "What's he doing here?" And for a long time, I asked myself the same thing.

I tried shrinking myself. I tried softening my voice, adapting my ideas, folding into shapes that would make others more comfortable. But here's the catch: no matter how small I made myself, it was never enough for them—and it was never right for me.

Then one day, something broke—but not in a bad way. Something cracked open. It wasn't a shout. It wasn't a grand rebellion. It was quiet. Subtle. A whisper from somewhere deep in my gut: "You don't need their permission to exist."

It was a strange kind of liberation—the kind that doesn't come with a celebration but with a reckoning. I realized I had been waiting. For years. Waiting to feel seen. Waiting to feel "ready." Waiting for someone—anyone—to say, "Yes, you belong here." But what if the very act of waiting was the thing keeping me small?

I began to study those who stood tall in a world that tried to push them down. And none of them waited for validation. The world didn't throw them welcome parties. It handed them silence, resistance, sometimes even hate—and still, they moved forward. What they had wasn't confidence. It was clear. The clarity that says: "Even if you don't understand me, I still get to be here."

So I stopped asking. I stopped waiting. I gave myself what the world refused to offer: permission.

I started walking into rooms like I belonged. Not arrogantly, but unapologetically. I began speaking my mind even when my voice trembled, even when my knees felt weak. And I'll tell you something strange: the world didn't explode. I wasn't struck down. In fact, some people started listening. Some doors creaked open. Not because I became someone new—but because I finally stood fully in who I already was.

The thing is, the world senses when someone has owned their worth. It's not loud, but it's unmistakable. You can feel it when someone walks into a room with quiet certainty—not the need to prove anything, but the presence of someone who knows they have nothing to prove.

I've seen people with more degrees than a thermometer who still doubt their voice. I've met people with none who shake the room when they speak. It's not about credentials. It's about conviction. You can't buy that in a bookstore. You can't borrow it from someone else. You have to build it. Brick by brick. Word by word. Choice by choice.

And don't get me wrong—I'm not saying recognition, applause, or support doesn't feel good. Of course it does. We're human. We all crave being seen. But if you live for applause, you'll die with its absence. External approval is the cherry, not the cake. Build the cake yourself. With your truth. With your defiance. With your fire.

That fire? It's inside you, right now. Maybe it's been dimmed. Maybe life, loss, or failure has tried to put it out. But it's still there, waiting. You don't need a standing ovation to light it again. You just need to stop asking, "Am I allowed to?" and start declaring, "I already am."

Let me be real: not everyone will clap when you rise. Some will be threatened. Some will mock. Some will ghost you, doubt you, belittle you. And that's okay. Let them sit in their smallness while you stand in your fullness. Your worth is not up for debate. It's a fact. Your existence is the proof.

People will try to measure you—by your grades, your salary, your looks, your "likes." But here's the thing: you're not a number. You're a force. And a force doesn't beg to be noticed. It moves with or without applause.

So own your name. Own your story. Own your scars and your stumbles and the strength it took to get here. Speak like you belong—because you do. Walk like the room is lucky to have you—because it is. Dream like the world's rules don't apply to you—because they don't.

You were born without permission. And that is your permission.

You don't need to become someone else to be worthy. You don't need to shrink to fit in. You don't need to earn your existence. You already have.

So the next time you walk into a room, don't wait for the nod. Don't scan for approval. Look straight ahead. Let them feel the quiet roar in your step. And if anyone asks who gave you the right to be here, look them in the eye and say:

"I did."

The Boy Who Scored Zero"

I still remember how it felt when I first realized I didn't belong. We had just moved to Nazirabad in Rajasthan. My dad was in the army, and moving every two years wasn't anything new to us—but this time, something was different. They put me in this international school. I was in the 5th grade. Everything around me felt like a world I wasn't prepared for. The kids were confident. They spoke fluent English like it was their first language, wore nice clothes, carried branded stuff, and always seemed to know what to say, when to say it. And me? I was just... there. New. Unsure. Trying to keep my head down and blend in.

The syllabus felt like it belonged to kids two or three years older than me. I wasn't catching up—I was just trying not to drown. I told people I was South Indian, and I could instantly feel the distance in how some of them looked at me. A few boys would sing "Appadi Podu" or yell movie lines from Gilli, trying to be funny. I laughed with them, but inside, I just felt smaller. They weren't bullying me exactly—it was just that subtle message that said: You're not one of us. It wasn't the jokes that hurt—it was the feeling that I didn't have a place. That if I disappeared the next day, no one would even notice.

Sanskrit was my worst subject. From day one, my teacher looked at me like I didn't stand a chance. She never said it outright, but I could feel it. That quiet disbelief. That unspoken "he's not going to make it." And maybe she was right—because I kept failing her subject, again and again. My mom was worried. She was proud of me, of course, but she didn't want me to be the kid who spoiled her name—especially because the school principal was her close friend. But my dad? He had a whole different take. He wasn't worried about reputation or image. One evening, when I was frustrated and ashamed, he looked at me and said, "Don't pass for anyone else. Don't do it for your mom. Learn it for yourself. If you fail, you fail. But don't run. Face it." That sentence cracked something open in me. He didn't sugarcoat it. He didn't comfort me. But he gave me something better—ownership.

After that, I stopped trying to survive quietly. I remembered this quote from Bruce Lee—"Be like water." Water doesn't resist. It doesn't argue. It adjusts, flows, finds a way. So that's what I did. I stopped waiting to be good enough and just started showing up. I raised my hand in class even when I didn't know the answer. I forced myself to speak, even if what I said sounded stupid. I gave wrong answers on purpose sometimes—just to train myself not to care. If I was going to get laughed at, so be it. Let it happen now, so it won't hurt later. And slowly, I got used to it. I stopped feeling shame. I stopped waiting for approval. I started showing up like I deserved to be there—even when I didn't feel it.

Then came the biggest hit. During the annual exam, I scored zero in Sanskrit. Not 10, not 20. Zero. It felt like the whole school knew the next day. People whispered in the hallways. "Who even gets a zero?" "Is that even possible?" I became a joke. Teachers gave me a look. The one where they don't say anything, but their silence says enough. My parents were called in. There were warnings. Lectures. Disappointment. I was humiliated. But for some reason—I wasn't destroyed. Because by then, I had already stopped living for their approval.

I had two friends—Karthik and Sushant—who stood by me. No judgment. No pity. Just presence. And that made a huge difference. Because even when the world laughs, all it takes is one or two people who still believe in you to keep going. I cleared the subject later, somehow. And from there, things started changing. Not overnight. Not magically. But slowly, consistently. My grades got better. My confidence grew. I started becoming someone else—or maybe I started becoming who I was all along.

By the time I got to 12th grade, people looked at me differently. Some thought I was smart, others thought I was just decent. But those who remembered me from 6th? They still saw the failure. The kid who got zero. But here's the truth—I stopped caring. Because I learned something most of them never did: your start doesn't define your ending. You can rewrite the whole thing if you choose to. You don't need anyone's permission to exist, to rise, to speak, to try.

That's what this chapter of my life taught me. I was never handed a title. I was never introduced as "brilliant" or "promising" or "gifted." I walked into rooms I wasn't invited to. I answered questions I wasn't supposed to raise my hand for. I became visible without anyone offering me the spotlight. And that's where the power is. Because when you stop waiting to be chosen—you start choosing yourself.

There's a big difference between identity and existence. Identity is something people try to put on you—labels, titles, grades, roles. But existence? That's yours. No one gives it to you. No one takes it away. You show up, you breathe, you try, you fail, you get back up. That's existence. That's what I learned.

I think of people like Muhammad Ali, who said, "I am the greatest" before the world believed him. Or Steve Jobs, who dropped out of college and still reshaped technology. Or Malala, who was told to stay silent, and chose to speak louder. None of them waited for permission. None of them waited for a certificate that said, "You're allowed now." They just were. They just did.

And that's what this chapter of my life is about. It's not about the grades. Not even the zero. It's about the moment I realized that no one was going to hand me my worth. That no one was coming to tap me on the shoulder and say, "Hey, you're enough now." I had to step into that on my own. Born without permission. But alive anyway. Loud anyway. Present anyway.

Because you don't need permission to belong. You don't need approval to begin. You don't need validation to breathe. And most of all—you don't need to be called worthy to know you are.

Identity vs Existence: Your Right to Take Space

The world loves its boxes. It needs to sort people to make sense of them—"topper," "failure," "reserved," "talented," "average," "not serious," "promising." It hands out these labels early, sometimes by the time you're in third grade, and then expects you to wear them like a second skin. But here's something they don't tell you when you're young: **you don't need a label to matter.** You don't need someone else to declare you "worthy" before you take your space in the world. You don't need to be called brilliant before you start learning like you are. You don't need to be named a leader to speak like one. You just need to show up—fully, audaciously, as you are. We've been fed the lie that our worth is something to be earned through applause, credentials, likes, trophies, gold medals. But the truth? Worth isn't earned. **It's inherited the moment you're born.**

Look around—does a lion wear a name tag that says "king"? Does it wait for the jungle to validate its roar? No. It takes space simply by existing. A storm doesn't carry a résumé. It doesn't walk into the sky and say, "Here are my qualifications." It just **happens**—loud, unapologetic, powerful. And you? You're no different. Stop waiting for a permission slip to be who you already are. You don't need someone to tap you on the shoulder and say, "Now you can take up space." You were always allowed. Always. Even when you failed. Even when they mocked you. Even when you were the punchline. Especially then. Because it's in those moments—when you feel unseen, unheard, underestimated—that your identity isn't being destroyed. It's being **forged.**

That zero I got in Sanskrit? It didn't define me. The whispers behind my back? They didn't shrink me. In fact, they did the opposite—they stripped away every external attachment I had to self-worth, and forced me to find value in my own breath, my own backbone. I stopped chasing titles. I started chasing the truth. And the truth was: **I belonged**, whether anyone said it or not. I didn't need to wait for my name to be called. I called it myself. Louder. Fiercer. Until I believed it. Until the room heard it too. Identity isn't about what others see when they look at you. It's about what you decide to become, even when no one's watching.

So no—I'm not the guy who waited in line for permission. I walked in, sat down, and made room. And if there wasn't space? I built my own damn table. You want to know what real identity is? It's not the title on your LinkedIn. It's how you carry yourself without one. It's how you speak when no one's listening. It's how you rise when no one's clapping. It's the way you own your name, your face, your scars, your voice—without explanation. And if someone asks, "Who gave you the right to be here?" you tell them this: **"I gave it to myself. I exist. That's enough."**

Quoting Rebels: Ali, Jobs, Malala
No legends asked for permission.

Let's talk about those who didn't wait for a green light. Let's talk about the ones who didn't stand in line—they kicked the damn door down.

Muhammad Ali didn't become the greatest and then say it. He said it first. Declared it loud, unapologetic, to a world that wasn't ready to hear it from a young, Black boxer with a mouth full of fire and fists to match. "I am the greatest," he said—long before anyone else would admit it. He didn't whisper it in a journal. He screamed it on microphones. And then he lived it. He danced, he jabbed, he fell, he rose. He lost some. He won the most. But through it all, his belief never flinched. Because greatness doesn't ask for permission—it walks in and *names itself.*

Steve Jobs? *That man got fired from his own company.* The very one he built. How's that for rejection? A college dropout, mocked for his weirdness, dismissed for his obsession with perfection, told over and over again that he was "too much." But he didn't shrink. He didn't compromise. He didn't beg for approval from people who couldn't see what he saw. He rebuilt. And he didn't just create better tech—he reshaped how we live. He showed us that brilliance doesn't come with straight edges and polite smiles. Sometimes, it comes in black turtlenecks, sleepless nights, and relentless belief in what can be.

And then there's **Malala**. A teenage girl with nothing but a backpack, a voice, and an unshakable will to learn. The Taliban shot her point blank for going to school. She should've disappeared. That's what they wanted. But instead, she came back with a story that pierced the world's conscience. She became louder. Stronger. Braver. She turned trauma into testimony. Fear into fuel. She took the bullet, and turned it into a mic. And the world finally listened.

Ali, Jobs, Malala—they couldn't have been more different. But they all had one thing in common: **they never asked for permission to matter.** They didn't wait for applause. They moved. Boldly. Imperfectly. Unapologetically. And the world? It caught up. Eventually.

So here's the takeaway: **Don't wait for permission to become who you already know you are.** Don't wait for the world to be ready for you—be ready for yourself. Be the one who walks in, owns the room, and says, "I'm not here to fit in. I'm here to be real."

IV

Born Without Permission

The first time I remember being praised, I was six. I had drawn a tree — just a simple green blob on top of a brown stick — but the teacher looked at it like I had painted the Mona Lisa. "Beautiful!" she said, showing it off to the class. My tiny chest puffed up. I smiled so hard it hurt. In that moment, I learned something no textbook ever taught: pleasing people feels good. The seed was planted. And like most seeds planted in childhood, it grew silently into the roots of my identity. Every compliment became a dose of dopamine. Every "good boy" wired me a little deeper into the idea that being liked equals being worthy. And so, I became likable. Not real. Not raw. Just... likable.

I did what was expected. I was polite even when I disagreed. I kept my head down even when I had questions. I smiled even when I wanted to scream. I was the safe kid, the dependable one, the "mature" one. I knew which parts of me the world clapped for — and which parts it didn't — so I adjusted. Edited. Masked. And at some point, the mask became the face. It didn't feel like a prison at first. In fact, it felt like luxury. Who wouldn't want to be admired? Who doesn't want the applause? But over time, I noticed something unsettling: the more people clapped for me, the more distant I felt from myself.

Praise, you see, is addictive. Not because it's bad, but because it's incomplete. It rewards surface behavior. It encourages repetition. But it rarely asks, "Is this truly you?" I was praised for getting good grades, so I became the top student. Praised for being respectful, so I never challenged authority. Praised for being easy-going, so I swallowed anger. And while the outside world clapped louder, inside, I was becoming hollow. Polished — but lost.

One of the deepest ironies of life is this: you can be celebrated for who you're not, and punished for who you truly are. The world often doesn't want your authenticity — it wants your agreement. Your consistency. Your predictability. And in chasing that acceptance, we trade something sacred — our voice. Our fire. Our weirdness. Our questions. And eventually, our truth.

It wasn't one big breakdown that woke me up. It was a series of tiny suffocations. I remember once being invited to speak at a small event. I gave a speech that I thought they wanted to hear. It was structured, polite, motivational — the kind of speech that makes people nod but not feel. They applauded. But I hated every second of it. It felt like betrayal — not of them, but of me. I had something deeper I wanted to say that day. Something raw. But I buried it under the polished version of me that everyone loved. And when I got off that stage, the applause rang in my ears like chains. That was the day I knew: if you build your life on applause, you will always live in fear of silence.

And silence... is necessary. Silence is sacred. Because it's only in silence that you hear your own soul. But when your entire self-worth is built on being liked, silence feels like death. So we keep talking. Performing. Pleasing. Until the version of us we've built is nothing but a reflection of everyone else's comfort zones.

"Urukku wasn't just steel. It was science before science had a name."

We often talk about the future as if it's something entirely new — as if human brilliance has only recently been unleashed by advancements in technology, algorithms, and artificial intelligence. But what if the truth is far different? What if, instead of discovering brilliance for the first time, we're merely **remembering** it? We're not uncovering something revolutionary; we are **reawakening** an ancient knowledge that once pulsed through villages, temples, and blacksmith shops. And few stories illustrate this more profoundly than the one hidden beneath the scorching heat of Tamilakam. This is a story not of laboratories filled with scientists, but of blacksmiths working by the glow of fire. Not of machines forging greatness, but of hands, heat, and heart. Not of accolades, but of truth. This is the forgotten story of **Urukku**, the extraordinary steel later known as **Wootz Steel.**

Urukku was not merely steel. It was **science before the word "science" even existed.** This steel was created in the deep South of India, centuries before the birth of Christ, and remains one of the earliest examples of **crucible steel** in human history. In places like **Salem, Madurai,** and **Tirunelveli,** artisans weren't crafting steel for fame or recognition — they were driven by a relentless pursuit of perfection. Their motivation wasn't about becoming viral; it was about doing something that could be **better, stronger, and more refined.** This wasn't just about metallurgy; this was a form of **knowledge passed down through generations,** a craft so perfected that it astonishes modern scientists to this day.

What these artisans didn't know was that the steel they created contained **carbon nanotubes** — a discovery that would not be made until the 20th century. Without microscopes or modern analytical tools, these Tamil blacksmiths had mastered a process of engineering at a **nano scale,** using **primitive yet ingenious techniques.** This steel was the core of the **legendary Damascus**

swords, blades so sharp that they could slice through other swords and remain razor-sharp over time. For centuries, European empires attempted to reverse-engineer the technique. They studied, tested, and experimented — but they could never replicate it. Because Urukku was not simply a material; it was the manifestation of a **deep, unbroken mastery of metalwork.**

And yet, this remarkable story has been largely forgotten. Urukku didn't fade into obscurity because it was ineffective. It was forgotten because the story **stopped being told.**

When the British colonized India, they didn't only take spices, textiles, and gemstones. They took knowledge. They infiltrated the very furnaces where this miraculous steel was created. But when they tried to replicate the craftsmanship in their industrialized factories, they failed. Unable to duplicate the quality of the steel, they dismantled the artisan systems. The forges were silenced. What couldn't be understood was erased. And for generations, we believed the myth that we were lagging behind. In reality, we had been **far ahead.**

Yet history has a way of whispering its truths back to us. Recently, scientists studying old Damascus blades were stunned to find microscopic **nanotube structures** inside them. They had expected corrosion. What they found instead were the same advanced features that Tamil blacksmiths had embedded into their steel long before the modern era had the tools to even recognize such things. Suddenly, the narrative shifted: Tamilakam didn't merely follow history; it led it.

We didn't follow the world.

We taught it.

We weren't behind in discovery.

We were early to mastery.

And most importantly — we created without the need for applause.

That is the fire we've lost in today's world.

We now live in a society where validation is everything. We wait for views, likes, and followers before we take action. We hesitate to take bold steps, not until we've received approval from an external source. The story of Urukku reminds us that the **greatest achievements** aren't driven by a desire for recognition. They are born from **a sense of purpose and an unwavering commitment to excellence.**

As I reflected on Urukku, I was reminded of the **Pyramids of Egypt.** Thousands of years old, yet still standing tall and perfectly aligned with the stars. Each stone weighs several tons, yet no cranes, no machinery, and no advanced technology were used in their construction. Today, scholars still debate how they were built. Some say it's impossible, others speculate extraterrestrial influence. But maybe the answer is simpler than that:

Maybe they built it because **no one told them it couldn't be done.**
Maybe they weren't trying to get recognition.
Maybe they weren't chasing trends.
Maybe they weren't looking for followers.
Maybe, like the blacksmiths of Tamilakam, **they were responding to a deeper calling.**

The Pyramids were raised in silence.
Urukku was forged in solitude.
And yet, both have **outlasted** every empire, every ruler, and every modern machine.

But today, we hesitated.
We wait for praise before we move.
We shrink our ideas to fit the approval of others.
We stifle our greatness, fearing it won't gain traction.
We suppress our dreams, worried they won't trend.

This is **The Prison of Praise** — a quiet cage we build for ourselves. One like, one comment, one applause at a time.

But your ancestors didn't wait.
They didn't ask for permission.
They didn't need validation.
They had **conviction.**

And now, it's your turn to remember who you are.

You don't need to be seen to be significant.

You don't need followers to lead.

You don't need praise to be powerful.

You come from **fire.**

Start anyway.

Let's pause for a second.

What do people clap for in you?

And more importantly — do those things feel like you?

Do they love your discipline... but not your dreams?

Do they admire your helpfulness... but never your honesty?

Do they call you mature... because you never disagree?

Do they like you because you're easy... not because you're real?

If yes, then maybe — just maybe — you're not being loved.

You're being managed.

And love is not management.

Here's what I've come to believe now:

Praise can be beautiful,

but it can also be a muzzle.

The world will clap for you

as long as you make them comfortable.

But the moment your truth

threatens their version of you,

the claps will stop.

Let them.

You are not a performer.

You are not applause furniture.

You are not someone's inspirational quote machine.

You are a wildfire.

And wildfires don't need permission to burn.

The Fallacy of "Perfect Timing" and the Courage to Be Different: Understanding That Growth Often Comes with Discomfort

We've all heard it before: "Wait for the perfect time." It's something many people say when they feel unsure about taking a big step. But here's the truth — the perfect time doesn't really exist.

It's a myth. And believing in it can stop us from moving forward. We often wait for the right conditions, for everything to fall into place, before we act. We wait until we feel completely ready, hoping that one day things will just click. But the reality is that nothing is ever perfect, and waiting for the perfect moment only causes us to miss chances.

The idea of perfect timing is really based on fear — fear of failure, fear of judgment, and even fear of success. We tell ourselves that once we feel more confident, more prepared, or more certain, we'll take action. But growth doesn't happen when everything is perfect. It happens when we push ourselves out of our comfort zone, even when things aren't ideal. Growth is messy. It's unpredictable. And it doesn't wait for everything to be just right.

Think about some of the important moments in your life. Were they perfect? Probably not. Yet, those are the moments that led to real change. Maybe you made a decision when you were uncertain, or you took a chance even though you didn't feel fully prepared. The chances are, those moments weren't "perfect." But they were still important because you took action. You grew because you did something, not because you waited for the perfect moment.

If we keep waiting for the perfect time, we might never do anything. The most meaningful accomplishments come when we take risks, when we step out of our comfort zone and act, even though we don't have all the answers. Life isn't about waiting for the perfect time — it's about moving forward despite the uncertainty. And that's when we start to grow.

Waiting for perfect timing is often just an excuse to avoid discomfort. We tell ourselves that we're not ready, that we need to know everything first. But life doesn't wait for us to be perfect. It keeps moving, and if we don't take action, we fall behind. So, the key isn't waiting for the perfect moment. It's taking action even when things feel uncertain. It's making the decision to move forward, even if we don't have everything figured out.

This brings us the courage to be different. Being different isn't always easy. In fact, it can feel uncomfortable. Society often pushes us to fit in, to follow the crowd, to do things the way everyone else does them. But the truth is, real growth comes from stepping away from the crowd and choosing your own path. It takes courage to be different — to do something that others might not understand or agree with. But it's only when we dare to be different that we truly create change.

When we choose to be different, we challenge the status quo. We question what we've been taught. We stop following the same paths that everyone else follows. And that's when we start to grow. It's uncomfortable to stand out. It's hard to be the person who doesn't fit in. But that discomfort is a sign of growth. When we push past the fear of judgment and embrace our uniqueness, we unlock our potential.

Think of people who have made a huge impact in the world. Many of them were different. They didn't wait for permission or approval to follow their passion. They trusted themselves and acted, even when it wasn't easy. They weren't afraid of being misunderstood or judged. They chose to be true to themselves, and that's what led them to success. The world needs more of that courage — the courage to be different, to challenge the norm, and to step into the unknown.

Growth often comes with discomfort. It's easy to think that growth should feel good, but that's not how it works. Growth happens when we push through challenges, when we take risks, and when we face things that scare us. It's when we choose to do the hard thing, the thing that makes us nervous, that we grow the most. We learn the most about ourselves during the tough times, not when everything is smooth and easy.

Take a moment and think about the things you've accomplished. Chances are, they didn't come without some discomfort. You might have had doubts, fears, or obstacles along the way. But it was through those challenges that you grew stronger. Growth isn't a straight line. It's filled with ups and downs. And the discomfort you feel when you step outside your comfort zone is a sign that you're on the right path. It means you're stretching, expanding, and becoming more than you were before.

So, the next time you feel like waiting for the perfect time or holding back because you're afraid to be different, remember this: There is no perfect time. And growth doesn't happen without discomfort. Embrace the discomfort. Step into the unknown. Trust yourself. You don't need everything to be perfect to start — you just need to take the first step. And remember, being different is not a weakness. It's a strength. It's the courage to break free from the norms and create something new, something real, something that only you can create.

The truth is, there is no perfect moment to start. The world will keep telling you to wait, to prepare, to be ready. But the reality is, growth happens when you step into the unknown, even when you feel unprepared. It's the discomfort that drives you forward, not the comfort of waiting for everything to align.

So stop waiting for the "perfect time" — because it doesn't exist. The perfect time is now. It's in the small actions you take, the risks you embrace, and the courage you find when you step outside your comfort zone. Remember, discomfort isn't a sign to stop; it's a sign that you're moving in the right direction.

And in those moments when you feel alone, or when you're walking a path that no one else understands, remember this: growth doesn't happen in the crowd. It happens in the quiet of your own courage, in the fire of your unique journey. You don't need the world to approve. You only need the courage to begin.

So go ahead — take the first step, even when you don't have all the answers. The discomfort you feel is simply the sign that you are growing, stretching, becoming more than you were before. And that is how real change happens — not in waiting, but in doing.

V

The Fire Doesn't Wait for Permission

There is a war within you. One side is loud, demanding, and relentless - it pulls you into every passing storm, every opinion shouted from a rooftop, every fear whispered in the corridors of conformity. This is the Noise. The other side is quiet - a murmur, a pull, a breath beneath the surface that you almost forget exists. This is the Voice. One distracts. The other directs. One is built by others. The other is born from you. And in the silence between their clash lies the life you were meant to live.

The Marketplace of Noise

We live in a marketplace of minds, each stall selling opinions dressed as truths. The sellers scream: Do more, be more, post more, prove more. Platforms buzz with filtered lives, carefully crafted for consumption, while algorithms decide what you should see, feel, and think. Everyone speaks, but few listen. Everyone reacts, but few reflect. It's not information overload - it's meaning starvation. We drown not because the world is too loud, but because we've forgotten what our own voice sounds like.

The Stoics warned of this centuries ago. Seneca wrote, "We suffer more in imagination than in reality." And yet, we construct our realities from imaginations, not even our own. Echo chambers reward sameness. Speed is mistaken for progress. Outrage is the new virtue. The Noise isn't just around us - it becomes us. It replaces the roots of conviction with vines of validation. But there is something deeper. Something ancient. Something untouched.

The Whisper in the Cave

Inside every human being is a sacred cave - a place untouched by applause, untouched by criticism. In this cave, there is a whisper. It does not beg for attention. It simply waits to be heard. This whisper is not always comforting. It may ask you to leave what is safe. It may tell you to walk alone. But it never lies. It knows who you are beneath the performance. It knows what breaks you and what builds you. It is the voice of your deepest self - the one that existed before the world told you who to be. In Plato's Allegory of the Cave, prisoners mistake shadows for truth because it's all they've ever known. When one breaks free and sees the sun, he realizes the illusion. But when he returns to tell the others, they mock him. They prefer the noise of shadows to the silence of light. The voice within is like that light - it shows you what is real, but it often isolates you from those who still worship the noise.

Echoes vs. Origins

The tragedy of modern life is not that we don't have voices - it's that we mistake echoes for them. Most thoughts we think are not truly ours. They're inherited, recycled, or implanted. We chase goals we never questioned. We seek praise we don't need. We run from failures that were never fatal. In chasing the echo, we abandon the origin. But the echo has no substance. It mimics. It is flattering. It distracts. The origin, though - the raw, trembling origin of your thoughts - that is where life begins.

Consider Galileo, who listened to the Voice even as the entire world shouted "heresy." His discoveries didn't come from consensus; they came from listening - not to the Noise of the church or noise - it was forged in listening. The crowd, but to the logic, the stars, and the quiet certainty within him. He was imprisoned for hearing what others refused to. But centuries later, it was his voice that remained - not theirs.

The Return to Stillness

To hear the voice again, one must become still. Not passive - still. Stillness is not the absence of action but the presence of clarity. Stillness allows the signal to separate from the static. In that stillness, you start to notice: not every urgency is real, not every demand deserves a response, not every voice is worth your energy. You learn to wait, to breathe, to listen beneath the surface. You begin to move from intention rather than reaction.

Meditation is one path. Solitude is another. But more than tools, it is a practice of remembering - remembering that you have always had access to this voice, that it never left, only got buried. The mystics called it Atman, the Hindus, the Self. The Bible called it the still small voice. The Buddhists saw it as right mindfulness. Each tradition, though separated by centuries and continents, speaks of the same truth: the voice is real, but it hides beneath the noise.

Voices That Built Civilizations

History remembers the voices, not the noise. It remembers Socrates, not his accusers. It remembers Martin Luther King Jr., not the letters that condemned him. It remembers Van Gogh, who painted not to please, but because the voice told him to. It remembers Rosa Parks, whose silence spoke louder than any speech. These were not perfect people. But they were people who listened. People who obeyed the voice, even when it cost them comfort, reputation, or life. Their legacy wasn't built in The pyramids weren't built with hashtags.

The Constitution wasn't drafted from trending opinions. The inventions, revolutions, and awakenings that shaped humanity were born not in reaction to the crowd, but in resistance to it. Greatness begins in a whisper - and is followed only by those willing to go deaf to everything else.

The Compass Within

You don't need another motivational quote. You don't need another five-step formula. You need to remember that the greatest compass already lives within you. Your voice is not a shout - it's a direction. It tells you not where to arrive, but where to begin. It won't promise comfort, but it will promise clarity. And clarity is more powerful than certainty. Because while the world changes its mind every minute, your voice always points north.

If you are to build something lasting - not just a career or a brand, but a life - you must learn to trust the voice over the noise. Not once. Not when it's convenient. But every single day. The world will give you a thousand reasons to abandon it. But even if you listen to it once, truly listen - you will never unhear it.

The Choice

Every morning, you are given a choice. You can plug in or tune in. You can scroll or you can sit. You can echo or originate. You can chase the noise or follow the voice. The first will give you applause, quickly. The second will give you peace, eventually. One fades. The other forms you.

VI

Bravery Isn't Loud

Every child is handed that same polished phrase—*"Reach for the stars."* It's stitched into classrooms, printed on motivational posters, and passed down like some universal gospel of ambition. But nobody tells you that the stars are surrounded by darkness. That in between here and there, there's nothing but long nights of silence, self-doubt, and moments when everything you thought you were shatters in front of you.

Nobody prepares you for the gravity—the force that pulls you down every time you try to rise. Nobody talks about the weight of expectation, the crushing silence after a public failure, the nights where sleep becomes your only escape from the voice in your head asking, "What if I'm not enough?"

They clap when you win. They repost your victory. They write articles after your success. But when you fall? When your plans explode in your face and you're left staring at the ashes? Most of them disappear. You'll scroll through your contacts and realize how many "supporters" were only ever spectators. People love a success story, but only when it's clean. They love a comeback, but only after you've showered, shaved, and scripted your speech. No one wants to sit in the wreckage with you. No one wants to look at your bruises while they're still bleeding.

But here's the truth nobody tells you—success isn't soft. It doesn't arrive gently, dressed in designer dreams and curated captions. Real success is ugly before it's beautiful. It's loud before it's celebrated. It's breakdowns in bathrooms. It's sleepless nights where your tears hit the pillow harder than your head ever could. It's screaming into the void, not because you're weak, but because you're still here.

This chapter? It's not for the ones who played it safe. It's not for the ones who coasted. It's for the ones who crashed. The ones who built something from nothing and then watched it fall apart. The ones who failed, not privately, but in front of everyone—on stages, in exam halls, in meetings, on timelines. And still chose to show up the next day.

This is the chapter before the TED Talk. The night before the viral post. The gut-wrenching, soul-splitting moment when you think, "Maybe this is it. Maybe I wasn't meant for more." And then, somehow, you get up.

Rising with dirt under your nails and scars on your chest. Rising with your name still shaking from the last failure, and saying it louder anyway. It's about choosing to rise when there's no crowd, no camera, and no certainty.

Because here's the brutal, sacred truth:

If your failure didn't echo in your soul, your rise will never shake the world.

And if you're going to rise—make sure they hear it.

The Volcano Doesn't Whisper

There's something sacred about destruction—something brutal, misunderstood, and essential. We are conditioned to fear it. From childhood, we're taught that destruction means failure, that to break is to lose, that anything burning must be put out before it causes damage. But nature tells a different story. Ask a geologist or someone who's watched the Earth split open—destruction is not the end. It's how new worlds are born. Look at volcanoes. They don't ask for permission. They don't creep in quietly. They explode. They tear through the sky, shatter the ground, and pour their insides onto the earth without apology. They are chaos incarnate. And yet, what comes after that chaos is not death. It's life.

After the eruption, when the dust settles and the molten earth begins to cool, something extraordinary happens. That scorched land becomes rich soil. That barren terrain becomes the birthplace of new ecosystems. Whole islands are formed from the ash of yesterday's destruction. Trees grow. Flowers bloom. Life begins. And not the same kind of life that existed before—but a life stronger, more vibrant, forged in fire. That is what failure is. Not just the collapse of something old, but the creation of something new. Something that couldn't exist without the violence of change.

But we're taught to hide our eruptions. To bottle them up. To be composed. Controlled. Gentle. We're taught to process our pain in silence, to break behind closed doors, to cry in bathrooms where no one can hear. We whisper our failures because we're scared of how they'll be received. But a volcano doesn't whisper. It doesn't hold back. And neither should you.

When you fail—when you fall so hard that your soul rattles—it's not proof that you're broken. It's proof that you're transforming. It's your eruption. The moment when the truth that's been buried deep beneath the layers of who you should be finally forces its way to the surface. And yes, it's messy. It's terrifying. It burns. But that burn is sacred. That destruction is necessary. You are not a robot meant to operate flawlessly. You are a force of nature. And forces of nature don't rise quietly.

The world keeps telling you that growth should be graceful. That healing should be linear. That ambition should be polite. But the reality is much more violent. Growth is often a war between who you are and who you're becoming. There will be nights where you scream into your pillow, wondering if it's all worth it. There will be mornings where your chest feels like it's caved in under the weight of your dreams. There will be seasons where everything you worked for crumbles—and everyone around you is watching. And in those moments, you'll be tempted to shrink. To disappear. To pretend the eruption never happened.

But don't. Don't apologize for your fire. Don't explain your breakdown to people who've never dared to build. Don't clean up your fall just to make it digestible for the world. You are not here to be palatable. You are here to erupt.

And in your eruption, there is power. Because the people who change the world are not the ones who play it safe. They're the ones who allow themselves to break, and then build something unrecognizable from the wreckage. They are the volcanoes, the wildfires, the thunderstorms—destructive in the moment, but essential in the grand scheme.

Your pain has a purpose. Your failure has a frequency. And the louder you allow it to be, the more room you make for others to find their voice too. Because when someone sees you own your eruption—when they see you rise from the lava, unashamed and still on fire—they remember that their own destruction doesn't have to be the end either. You give them permission. Not by being perfect, but by being *real*.

There is a reason ancient cultures worshipped volcanoes. They understood the duality: the danger and the divinity. They feared them, yes, but they also revered them. Because deep down, they knew what we keep trying to forget—*that fire is not the enemy.* Fire clears the old. Fire makes way for rebirth. Fire refines. And fire, when wielded right, doesn't just destroy—*it creates.*

So let your failures burn. Let them roar. Let them melt away everything that no longer serves you. Let them strip you down to your core so that you can rise, not as a replica of someone else's idea of success, but as a force that cannot be ignored. A volcano does not erupt because it wants attention. It erupts because pressure makes staying the same impossible. And maybe that's where you are right now—not broken, but pressurized. Not lost, but on the edge of transformation.

The next time you fall apart, don't ask how to fix it. Ask what it's making space for. Ask what version of you is trying to be born from the ash. Stop trying to tidy your growth. Stop editing your pain into something polite. Be loud. Be messy. Be molten. Be the kind of person who rises from a breakdown with ash still on their skin and purpose in their eyes.

The Samurai Who Failed With Honor

In the spring of 1185, the world knew how the story would end. Minamoto no Yoshitsune, a brilliant young samurai general, stood on the edge of defeat. Not because he was weak. Not because he lacked strategy or strength. But because the world had turned against him. He was betrayed by those he trusted, cornered by political tides beyond his control, and hunted down by the very man whose wars he had helped win—his own half-brother, Yoritomo. It wasn't just a battle he was fighting. It was a reckoning.

Yoshitsune had every reason to run. To surrender. To plead for mercy. Most men in that position would've taken the quiet way out—disappear, submit, or die in silence. But Yoshitsune was not like most men. He wasn't built to exit history quietly. So even when every military advantage was gone, when his allies had turned into enemies and his escape routes were erased, he did what very few ever do in the face of certain failure—he chose to fight anyway.

He didn't fight to win. He knew the war was lost. He fought because his story deserved a warrior's end, not a whisper. He tightened his grip on his sword, mounted his horse, and led what was left of his loyal warriors into battle—not for victory, but for dignity. And he lost. He fell. But his fall became thunder.

Yoshitsune's death was not just remembered—it was immortalized. His legend grew larger than his victories ever could have. The Japanese wrote songs about him. Scholars studied him. His life became theatre. Statues were carved in his image, not because he was perfect, but because he dared to fall without hiding. He became a symbol of something that transcends winning: honor in failure. Fire in defeat. The art of losing with your chin up and your sword still raised.

You see, there's a type of failure the world respects—even reveres. It's the kind where you don't retreat, even when retreat makes sense. The kind where you bleed publicly and don't flinch. The kind where you lose, but on your own terms. That's what Yoshitsune represents. Not flawless victory—but glorious collapse. Not the final score—but the courage it takes to play the game knowing you're outmatched.

In today's world, we're so obsessed with winning that we've forgotten how to fail properly. We hide our losses. We sugarcoat our setbacks. We pretend the moments that broke us didn't happen. Social media doesn't show you the breakdown—it filters it out, puts a quote over it, and posts the rebound. But let me be clear: sanitized failure is forgettable. It's the ugly, exposed, honest failure that people remember. The kind you don't clean up. The kind you walk through in full view.

You want to live a story that echoes? Then don't just win. Be willing to lose loudly. Like Yoshitsune. Because in the end, nobody builds statues for people who disappeared quietly. They built them for the ones who went down swinging.

Here's the deeper truth no one tells you—winning isn't always in your control. You can do everything right and still lose. You can plan, prepare, sacrifice, and bleed, and still not get what you were chasing. But how do you lose? That's fully yours. That's your fingerprint at the moment. That's where your character isn't crafted—it's revealed.

When you fail with honor, people don't see the fall. They see the fire. And fire sticks with people. That's why Yoshitsune is remembered after nearly 900 years. Not because he was undefeated—but because he refused to surrender his spirit. Because he fell with his whole chest. Because he walked into that final battle with his story unfinished, but his pride intact.

Most people in life are afraid of failing at all, let alone failing publicly. That fear makes them small. It silences their ambition. It convinces them to quit before they begin. But what if we started treating failure not as a mark of shame—but as proof of movement?

What if, instead of trying to avoid defeat, we tried to master the art of falling well? Yoshitsune didn't just fall—he choreographed it like a warrior's ballet. There was poetry in how he lost. Purpose in the way he didn't retreat.

And maybe that's what we need more of in this world—not perfect records, but perfect resolve.

So if you're going to fail—and you *will*—fail like a damn legend. Don't edit it. Don't shrink from it. Don't explain it away. Own it. Let people watch. Let it be loud. Let your story be unignorable, even when the ending isn't a victory.

We need more people like Yoshitsune today. People who don't wait for permission to act, who don't crumble under betrayal, who don't dilute their flame to fit into the world's expectations. People who walk into defeat wearing their full truth. Who fights anyway, even when the scoreboard is rigged. Who says, *"If I'm going down, I'm going down in fire."* That's the kind of failure that time can't erase. Because that's what failure is supposed to be: Louder than your excuses. Louder than the silence that follows defeat. Loud enough to shake time itself.

The Brutality of Becoming: Whiplash

There's a scene in *Whiplash* that sticks to your ribs. Not because of the jazz or the technique, but because of what it costs the main character—Andrew—to chase greatness. You see him drenched in sweat, hands blistered and bleeding, slamming the drums like his life depends on it. And in a way, it does. He's not just playing music. He's being torn apart. Rebuilt. Burned into something new. His teacher, Fletcher, is relentless—borderline monstrous. He doesn't offer praise. He doesn't offer rest. He throws chairs, screams in faces, humiliates. Not because he hates his students, but because he hates mediocrity.

And somewhere in that brutality, you start asking yourself the same uncomfortable question: **What does it really take to be great?**

Most people don't want to hear the answer. Because the answer isn't kind. It isn't clean. The answer is sacrifice. Isolation. Rejection. The answer is sitting in a dark room, perfecting something no one cares about yet. It's failing, again and again, without anyone clapping. It's falling apart in front of people and showing up anyway. And the most haunting part? The world will ignore you until you're undeniable. And when you finally break through, they'll pretend they believed in you the whole time.

There's a line in *Whiplash* that deserves to be tattooed across every dreamer's heart:

"There are no two words more harmful than 'good job.'"

"Good job" is the participation trophy of language. It's what we're handed when we've done just enough to not get fired, just enough to pass, just enough to get by. It's disguised as encouragement, but it's actually a sedative. It lulls us into thinking we've arrived when we've only just begun. It's the way society teaches you to plateau. To the coast. To settle.

We hand out "good jobs" like candy, and then we wonder why greatness feels extinct. We hand out praise for average work, then expect people to suddenly be extraordinary under pressure. It doesn't work that way.

Because greatness? Greatness is allergic to comfort.

Greatness doesn't happen in applause—it happens in silence. In rejection letters. In practice rooms where no one is watching. In moments where your body wants to give up, but your soul refuses. It happens when you play until your hands bleed, not because someone told you to, but because something inside you won't shut up. That's the brutality of becoming. It doesn't just hurt your body. It slices into your identity. It shatters who you thought you were, and demands that you build someone new out of the rubble.

Andrew doesn't just bleed on those drums—he transforms. He sheds the skin of the boy who wanted approval and becomes the man who demands greatness from himself. He stops needing permission. He stops chasing validation. He stops trying to be liked. And that's the moment everything changes. Not when he gets the notes right, but when he becomes something unbreakable.

Whiplash is not a story about music. It's a story about obsession. About how far someone is willing to go to become unforgettable. And not everyone agrees with the method. Fletcher is cruel. He crosses lines. He breaks people. But his philosophy is simple: if a person is truly destined for greatness, nothing—not rejection, not pain, not humiliation—will stop them. The pressure will either destroy them or reveal them. There's no middle ground.

And maybe that's the ugly truth we all need to swallow: **Comfort is the enemy of greatness.**

You don't become exceptional by being liked. You don't grow by being coddled. You don't evolve by being told you're good enough. You grow when you're stretched past your limits. When life slaps you so hard that your only options are to quit or become someone new. That's the fire. That's where the alchemy happens. Not in praise, but in pain.

We live in a culture addicted to convenience. Everyone wants to go viral. Everyone wants to be an "overnight success." But no one wants to bleed for it. No one wants to live in the shadows, honing their craft while everyone else gets the spotlight. No one wants to be pushed past their limits, even though that's the only place real transformation exists.

You want to be great? Then let it hurt. Let it wreck you. Let it strip you of every false layer until only the real you remains. And don't run from that pain. Don't numb it. Don't hide it behind curated captions and clean aesthetics. Because pain, when you let it shape you instead of shame you, becomes power. That's what *Whiplash* teaches. And it's terrifying. Because it forces you to confront the question:

Do I actually want to be great, or do I just want to be comfortable?

If it's comfort you're after, then "good job" will do. Collect your gold stars. Post your highlight reel. Stay safe. But if it's greatness you're chasing—then get ready to suffer. Not for drama. Not for pity. But because transformation demands blood. So pick up your drumsticks—whatever that means for you. Bleed on them. Sweat on them. Practice when no one's watching. Embrace the teacher who's hard on you. Walk into the spaces that scare you. Chase the note that feels impossible. And when the world says "good job," don't let it seduce you. Don't let it lull you to sleep.

My Loudest Fall

I still remember the sting of that failure as if it happened yesterday.

I was sixteen when I failed the National Defence Academy exam. It wasn't a simple stumble. It wasn't a narrow miss. It was a full collapse—a crushing blow to everything I had built up in my mind. I had spent months preparing, but it wasn't enough. It wasn't just an exam; it was a dream I hadn't prepared for, not truly. I had romanticized it, made it feel like the answer to everything, but I hadn't fought for it with the grit it demanded. The shame wasn't only in failing—it was in the realization that I hadn't earned the right to succeed. That hurt deeper than any result could.

We were living in Punjab at the time, but I chose to take the exam in Bangalore—my hometown. The decision wasn't just about the exam center; it was about something bigger. It was about coming back home a hero. My family and I booked flights, made travel arrangements, and with every step, there was an air of expectation—like a celebration before the race even started. They believed in me. They had visions of me returning victorious, as though the victory was a given. The red carpet of life was rolled out, but I hadn't earned it yet. I had imagined it, sure, but I hadn't truly worked for it.

When I finally sat down in that exam hall, everything hit me at once. The air in the room felt thick, and my chest tightened. The numbers on the paper blurred into an indecipherable mess. What should've been familiar was now a strange code. My brain froze in panic, and all the preparation I had done felt irrelevant. My entire foundation—my study, my plans, my rehearsed confidence—crumbled under the weight of reality. I could sense my failure before the results even came. It wasn't just the exam; it was my entire approach to it. I wasn't ready. I hadn't truly been prepared to face it.

When the results were released, I already knew. But it didn't make the silence any less deafening. I had let my family down. They had pinned so many hopes on this, traveled all the way for it. The look in their eyes when I told them I had failed was almost more painful than the failure itself. But to my surprise, they didn't scold me. They didn't express disappointment. Instead, they said:

"If you can dream it, then you should achieve it. It's not a big deal that you failed. There are many paths to what you want. You just have to keep walking." Those words... they didn't heal me immediately. They didn't patch up my broken pride or erase the bitter taste of failure. But they did something far more profound: they transformed me.

That moment marked the first time I met myself—not as the one who succeeds, but as the one who endures. Not the person who wins, but the one who rises every time they fall. It was a humbling revelation. I realized then that success doesn't define you. What truly defines you is your ability to keep going when everything is against you. The world doesn't remember how you fell. It remembers how you got back up. Failure, especially the loud kind, doesn't end you. It births you into something more resilient, something unshakable. And that's the power I didn't realize I had until that moment. It's not about the fall—it's about the rise.

Echo Failures vs. Origin Failures

Not all failures are created equal, Some are silent collapses—the kind that barely leave a mark. These are **Echo Failures**. They sound like everyone else. They look like a borrowed dream dressed in your body. You followed the checklist. You wore the suit. You repeated someone else's formula. You did what was expected. You played it safe. You walked a path already proven.

The world doesn't mourn those failures. Hell, the world barely notices. Because when you echo someone else's life, even your collapse feels muted. Forgettable. Replaceable. That's the danger of playing small and safe: when you fall, it doesn't even make a sound.

Origin Failures

The kind that erupts straight from your gut. The kind where you dare to create something the world hasn't seen yet. Where you take your ideas—unpolished, imperfect, on fire—and throw them into the universe, knowing damn well they might burn. And sometimes, they do. They crash but they crash with your fingerprint on them.

Because even in destruction, there is identity. There is ownership. There is creation. Origin failures don't whisper. They make the ground shake. They leave debris that eventually becomes blueprints. They are not pretty, but they are real. Raw. Undeniably you.

Think about every person who changed the game—scientists, artists, revolutionaries, misfits. They didn't start with success. They started with chaos. With the kind of failure that looked like madness to everyone else. They were told "No one will understand this," and they still went ahead. They failed not because they were wrong—but because they were early. Too original for the room they were in. Every invention? Origin failure. Every paradigm shift? Origin failure. Every voice that ever cracked open a new way of thinking? Failed. Loudly. Publicly. Beautifully.

So ask yourself—when your plans fall apart, when your ideas flop, when your voice shakes and the room goes silent—was it because you echoed someone else's path?

- Echo failures are forgotten.
- Origin failures become foundations.

Letter to My Younger Self

Dear Me,

I know it hurts.

The fall. The silence. The look in their eyes when you didn't make it.

Don't turn away from the pain.

Look at it. Let it cut. Let it sting. Let it brand you.

This is not punishment. This is a door.

Walk through it.

Don't tiptoe.

Crash through it like you own the other side.

And when you rise, don't be quiet about it.

Be thunder.

Your future self is already clapping.

You can rise quietly and be forgotten, or you can rise with thunder and be unforgettable. The choice is yours: blend into the background or make a lasting impact. And if you're going to fail, don't do it silently fail loud. Let your setbacks echo with the lessons they've taught. Then, rise louder.

VII
The Mirror Is a Battlefield

It begins in silence. A stare. A glance. A pause so small the world doesn't notice, but your soul does. You stand in front of the mirror, and suddenly, it's not just glass reflecting your image—it's a warzone. Not of bombs or bullets, but of beliefs, of whispered doubts, of scars that don't bleed but burn. The mirror doesn't lie, but it doesn't always tell the truth either. What it shows is not the body, but the battleground between how the world has shaped you and how you see yourself. The mirror becomes the cruelest stage—a performance you never auditioned for, judged not by others, but by the harshest critic of all: you. Every wrinkle becomes a failure. Every scar, a flaw. Every imperfection, a reason to shrink. The war isn't against the reflection—it's against the noise that shaped what you think it means.

The first time you ever looked into a mirror as a child, you didn't see failure. You didn't compare. You didn't criticize. You smiled. You laughed. You poked your own cheeks and tilted your head like a curious little explorer marveling at their own existence. That child saw wonder. That child saw magic. And then came the voices. "You should lose weight." "You're too dark." "You're not tall enough."

"Why are your teeth like that?" And with each comment, each sneer disguised as advice, the child in the mirror faded—and the soldier stepped in. A soldier who now stands daily in front of the mirror, armor cracked, sword shaking, ready to fight ghosts of opinions that never belonged to them. The mirror became a battlefield not because of how we looked, but because of how we were told to look.

Every advertisement, every magazine, every filter-fed photo tells you what "beautiful" should be. And every time you don't see that in your reflection, you declare war on yourself. But here's the truth no one ever tells you—beauty was never meant to be copied, it was meant to be owned. The oak doesn't envy the rose, and the lion never compares its mane to the eagle's wings. But humans, armed with fragile egos and manufactured ideals, look into a mirror hoping to see someone else. And when we don't, we punish ourselves. We forget that confidence isn't found in the mirror—it's felt in the fire behind our eyes. Yet we keep returning to that glass altar, hoping one day, we'll be enough.

I once stood before a mirror the night before a big speech. My hands trembled. Not because I doubted my message—but because I doubted the messenger. "Who are you to speak to?" the voice whispered. "You're just a boy from a small town. You don't look like a leader." And for a moment, the mirror won. I almost canceled. But something inside me snapped. A deeper voice—a quieter, fiercer one—rose and said, "It's not about what you look like. It's about what you stand for." I spoke anyway. And that night, I won my first battle. Not on stage, but in the mirror.

Mirrors have no memory, but we do. Every time we stand in front of them, we bring every insult, every shame, every time we were made to feel 'less than.' We project those wounds onto our reflection and call it reality. But the battlefield can be reclaimed. The mirror can be made sacred again—not a place of shame, but of power. It starts when we stop looking for flaws and start looking for fire. When we start asking not "how do I look?" but "who do I choose to be today?" The mirror doesn't get to answer that. You do.

There's a reason warriors stare at their reflection before battle. It's not vanity—it's grounding. A reminder of purpose. A declaration of identity. And maybe that's what we need to reclaim. Not the mirror, but the meaning. What if every time you looked into the mirror, you didn't inspect yourself—you introduced yourself? "This is who I am. This is what I believe. This is the fire I carry." Not for perfection, but for presence. Not to impress, but to express. Because when you own your reflection, the world has no choice but to respect your presence.

You will lose some battles. There will be days you look in the mirror and feel small. Tired. Broken. But even on those days, especially on those days, look again. Not at your skin, or your shape, or your shadows. Look at your story. Look at your survival. Look at the spark that still burns behind your tired eyes. And if you see even a flicker, you haven't lost. Not yet.

The mirror is a battlefield. But it's also a canvas. A window. A friend, if you let it be. You are not your flaws. You are not your scars. You are the fire that rises anyway. The voice that speaks anyway. The soldier who shows up, again and again, armed not with perfection, but with purpose. The mirror doesn't define you. You define the mirror.

We were never taught to see ourselves—we were trained to judge ourselves. From school photos to locker room mirrors, from Instagram filters to wedding-day critiques, the reflection became a report card. And the standards? Ever-changing, unforgiving, unreal. You were either too much or not enough. Too loud or too quiet. Too skinny, too heavy. Too dark, too pale. Too plain, too "trying too hard." The problem was never the mirror—it was the metric. It was the lie that your worth could be measured by symmetry or shape, by how others react when they see you. What if the mirror never needed fixing—what if the eyes looking into it did?

Some cultures believed mirrors could trap souls. That they were portals, gateways to another realm. And in a way, they were right. Because when you stand in front of a mirror long enough, something does get trapped: your truth. You start to perform for your own reflection. You pose, you flex, you suck in, you tilt. Not for yourself, but for the image of the person you think you're supposed to be. You become an actor in your own life, rehearsing lines like "I'm fine," "I'm doing great," "This looks good, right?" The tragedy is, the more you pose, the more your real self fades. And the mirror? It just watches, quietly, as another soul trades authenticity for approval.

There's a story from Japanese legend—of the samurai who stared into polished bronze mirrors before battle. Not to admire their face, but to confront their fears. The mirror was a ritual, a sacred pause. A warrior would stand still, face his own reflection, and ask: Am I ready to die for what I believe in today? It wasn't vanity. It was a vision. And that's the kind of reflection we've forgotten. Not one of appearance, but of alignment. Not "Do I look good?" but "Do I recognize myself?" We need mirrors that ask better questions. Mirrors that don't just reflect bodies, but call out souls.

But instead, we built temples for appearance. Social media became the mass-market mirror—fast, addictive, and never satisfied. Every scroll whispers, You should look like this. Be like that. Edit more. Show less. Smile wider. And so we obey. We filter. We hide. And slowly, we lose the raw, powerful image of ourselves we were born with. A baby doesn't need filters. A child doesn't pose. They dance in front of mirrors, make faces, laugh wildly. Until one day, someone tells them to stop. "Don't be silly." "Look proper." "Stand straight." And just like that, the war begins.

Yet here's the paradox: The world only sees you through the lens you first choose to see yourself. If you walk into a room shrinking, apologizing for existing, the world will not fight you on it. It will let you shrink. It will reward your silence. But if you stand before the mirror, meet your own gaze, and refuse to flinch, something changes. That's how revolution begins—not in parliaments or protests—but in private, sacred confrontations with your own reflection.

I once met a boy who hated photographs. He'd turn away, lower his head, or force a smile so strained it looked painful. When I asked him why, he said, "Because I don't want to see how far from perfect I am." That sentence hit like a blade. Not because it was rare—but because it was familiar. We all carry a version of that boy inside us. A voice that tells us, "Don't look too closely. You might find everything wrong." And yet, he wasn't wrong about himself—he was wrong about the mirror. Because the mirror doesn't show what's wrong. It shows what is. It's we who decide whether "what is" is enough. And sadly, most of us were taught to see ourselves as a problem to fix, not a miracle to protect.

There's a haunting irony in our generation: we take more photos than any in history, but we hate being seen. We obsess over lighting, angles, and filters, not because we're vain—but because we're afraid. Afraid that the raw, unfiltered version of us might not be accepted. Might not be worthy. We spend hours retouching pixels but never spend minutes retouching our beliefs. We invest in serums and surgery but rarely invest in silence—the kind that lets us sit with ourselves, truly, without judgment. Because silence is uncomfortable. It echoes. It reveals. And in that quiet space between glances, we're forced to admit: the war in the mirror was never about appearance. It was always about acceptance.

And yet, how cruel it is that the world celebrates mirrors that lie. We're sold reflections of perfection, curated to the edge of inhuman. Airbrushed beauty, frozen smiles, impossible bodies—these become the gold standard. Not because they are real, but because they're repeated. Repetition builds belief. And belief shapes vision. So when you stand in front of a mirror and don't see what the world praises, the mind turns brutal. "Why don't you like them?" it asks. And the answer becomes a list of imagined inadequacies. And still, we forget the obvious truth—you were never supposed to be like them. You were supposed to be like you.

What if we stopped standing in front of mirrors waiting to feel beautiful—and instead stood in front of them to remember we are becoming? Becoming is messy. Becoming is imperfect. But becoming is powerful. It's not about arriving at an image the world approves of—it's about arriving at a self you no longer have to hide from. And when that shift happens—when you look in the mirror and don't attack, don't flinch, don't wish to swap places with someone else—you've won a battle most people will never even realize exists.

The mirror is not a battlefield because it reflects flaws. It's a battlefield because it forces confrontation with truth. And truth is uncomfortable. But here's the promise: the more truth you can face in the mirror, the more truth you can carry into the world. And truth, unlike beauty, cannot be photoshopped. It can only be lived.

There's a myth from ancient Greece that echoes through every bathroom and selfie: the tale of Narcissus. A man so captivated by his own reflection in still water that he forgot to live. He stared endlessly, falling in love with the image, until he died beside it. The world tells this story as a warning against vanity. But they miss the deeper truth: Narcissus didn't die because he loved himself too much—he died because he didn't recognize that the image wasn't him. He fell for a symbol, an illusion, a trap. And that is the same fate we risk when we confuse reflection with reality. When we confuse surface with soul. Narcissus drowned not in water—but in the lie that a reflection holds more value than the life beyond it.

But not all cultures treated the mirror as a tool of vanity. In many African tribes, mirrors were spiritual objects. They were not placed on walls but stored carefully, sometimes hidden. Because it was believed that a mirror could reflect not just the face—but the spirit. They knew what we've forgotten: that looking into a mirror is a sacred act. That how you see yourself shapes how you walk, how you speak, how you rise. If your mirror is cracked, your spirit limps. If your mirror is fogged by comparison, your path becomes blurred. But when the mirror is clean—cleansed by truth, by inner clarity—you don't just see yourself... you meet yourself.

In some Native American traditions, young warriors were given polished stones or reflective surfaces not to judge their looks, but to seek vision. To ask, "What am I becoming?" before battle, before leadership, before love. The reflection was a starting point—not a verdict. It wasn't a question of "Am I good enough?" but "Am I aligned enough?" Are my actions reflecting my spirit? Is the outside mirroring the inside? Imagine if we asked that instead of "Do I look okay today?"

But in today's world, we don't use mirrors as windows to the soul—we use them as weapons. And the first casualty is always confidence. How many dreams died because someone looked in the mirror and didn't like what they saw? How many stories were never written, songs never sung, hands never raised, because the person holding the pen or mic or possibly first looked at their reflection and said, "Not good enough." And what if they were wrong? What if the mirror lied? Or worse, what if their beliefs were the real distortion?

There is no such thing as a "perfect" reflection—because perfection doesn't reflect, it projects. It's a fantasy. A still frame in a world that is meant to move, evolve, and grow. What matters most isn't what the mirror shows, but what you choose to see. And seeing is a skill. A sacred one. Not learned through filters or fashion, but through fierce honesty and radical acceptance. Because once you master how you see yourself, no one else's view can define you.

The mirror is not glass—it is a question. A silent, relentless question: "Who are you becoming?" And most days, we answer that question not with words, but with reactions. We look and we flinch. We adjust. We frown. We critique. And in those tiny moments, we don't just change our posture—we shape our destiny. Because if every glance in the mirror teaches you to dislike yourself, you will move through the world as if you are unworthy of being seen. And you'll overcompensate. You'll chase praise like oxygen. You'll stay silent in rooms where your voice is needed. You'll become what is acceptable, not what is authentic. And nothing is more painful than living inside a body that feels like a costume you didn't choose.

But what if, one day, you refused to flinch? What if you stood still, barefaced, unfiltered, and said, "This is me. This is mine. And it is enough." Not as a weak mantra, but as a battle cry. Because self-acceptance isn't soft—it's rebellious. In a world that profits from your insecurity, loving yourself is a form of resistance. You were told confidence is earned, but that's a lie. Confidence is reclaimed.

It was yours the moment you were born. You just forgot. Or more truthfully, you were taught to forget.

Look at children. Give them a mirror and they don't flinch. They dance. They roar. They experiment. They are not performing—they are playing. And that's the word we lost. Play. Because the mirror became a courtroom, not a canvas. But imagine reclaiming it. Imagine waking up, walking to the mirror, and using it like the ancient warriors did—not to judge, but to align. To check: Does this face reflect my fire? Does this expression carry my story? Is the person in the mirror the one I fought to become, or the one I've been hiding behind?

And then you realize: the battlefield was never just about image—it was about permission. Who gave you permission to stand tall? Who gave you permission to feel beautiful, or powerful, or enough? The world won't hand you that permission—it will hand you products, promises, conditions. But the mirror? The mirror waits for you to give it. Because when you do—when you finally say, "I see you, and I won't apologize for you"—you don't just win the war. You end it.

There is a quiet revolution that starts not in protests, not in speeches, but in the simple, everyday act of refusing to self-abandon. That's what the mirror tests most. Not beauty. Not symmetry. But loyalty—to yourself. Every time you look into that glass and reject what you see, you are telling your soul, "I choose the world's opinion over yours." And you do it enough times, and your soul... stops speaking. That inner voice that once told you to create, to speak, to try, to leap—it dims. Not because it's gone. But because it no longer trusts that you're listening.

But you can earn it back. Not through appearance, but through alignment. Through fierce self-trust. It begins with one look in the mirror where you say, "I may not be where I want to be, but I am not abandoning who I am to get there." That kind of look rewires something deep. It reclaims your body as your own. It makes your face feel like home, not a battlefield. And when that happens, the mirror doesn't become irrelevant—it becomes sacred.

Here's the strange thing: those who carry deep self-acceptance... they don't need the mirror anymore. They check it, sure. They might smile at it, adjust a collar, nod with quiet pride. But they are not dependent on it. Because their reflection lives elsewhere—in how they speak, how they love, how they walk into a room without shrinking. And the world feels it. Confidence is invisible, but it is undeniable. It doesn't need a mirror—it becomes one. People look at someone who truly accepts themselves, and they begin to wonder if they can do the same.

And that's how you change the world: one reflection at a time. Not by convincing others to see you differently, but by choosing to see yourself differently, first. The mirror is the first gate. The first confrontation. And once you pass through it, you realize: your body was never a billboard. Your face was never a canvas for their approval. You were never designed to be pleasing—you were designed to be true. And the truth is rarely polite. It is rarely neat. But it is always powerful.

So maybe the next time you stand before the mirror, don't ask, "How do I look?" Ask, "Am I being loyal to who I am?" Because that question changes everything. That question turns the battlefield into a sanctuary.

The mirror is not just where you face your reflection. It's where you face your beliefs. Beliefs you didn't choose—but inherited. From comments said in passing. From magazines. From cruel schoolyard jokes. From a mother who never liked her own face. From a father who never said "You're enough." From silent lessons carved into you by a world that teaches worth as a shape, a shade, a size, a softness. So when you stand before the mirror, you're not just seeing yourself. You're seeing a collision of expectations. You're staring at a gallery of ghosts: what they wanted you to be, what they feared you might become, what you tried to escape. But somewhere in the center of all that noise... is you. The original. Untouched. Waiting.

And the war begins the moment you try to dig her out. Because reclaiming your real self means disappointing someone. It means saying, "I won't play this game anymore." And that's terrifying.

Because the world does not reward authenticity—it tests it. It asks, "Are you sure?" over and over, in different disguises. It pushes shame through compliments. It wraps comparison in friendship. It puts likes and comments in place of self-worth and then calls it love. But if you hold your ground—if you look in the mirror and choose to see truth over trend—you start to win. Quietly. Fiercely. Without applause.

Because here's what no one tells you: the mirror remembers. Every time you choose kindness over criticism, it softens. Every time you meet your eyes instead of your flaws, it shifts. The glass becomes clearer. Not because you've changed how you look—but because you've changed how you see. The battlefield becomes a place of reunion. You meet the self you were before they told you who to be. And that self? She's strong. Not because she's never been hurt—but because she knows how to rise without armor.

And in that moment, when the mirror stops being your enemy—you don't need to win anything anymore. You've already won. Because the greatest victory isn't in looking perfect. It's in looking at yourself... and not flinching.

There comes a moment, often quiet and unnoticed, when the war ends. Not because the mirror changes, but because you do. Because you finally stop waiting for a different reflection and start building a different relationship—with yourself. It doesn't happen in a grand gesture. It happens when you stop apologizing for taking up space. When you put down the foundation that never matched your skin. When you wear the outfit you love, not the one that hides. When you speak and don't shrink. When you look into your own eyes and don't ask for permission. That is the beginning of freedom—not the kind sung in anthems, but the kind whispered in front of mirrors at midnight.

Because the battlefield was never about image. It was about identity. It was about the right to define yourself in a world that constantly tries to do it for you. And the mirror—poor, innocent mirror—was never the enemy. It just reflected whatever war was raging inside. And now? Now it reflects your return. You're rising.

Your reclamation.

You'll still have bad days. You'll still catch your reflection sideways and feel that old sting. But now you'll recognize it for what it is: a scar, not a sentence. A memory of who you used to be—not a command to become her again. Because you've met yourself now. And once you've met your real self—the unfiltered, unashamed, unshakeable self—you can't unsee her. You can't go back to mirrors as measuring tapes. You start using them as altars.

Yes—altars. A sacred space where you check in, not check boxes. A space where you remind yourself: "This face has faced so much, and still... it faces forward." Where the question is no longer "Do I look worthy?" but "Am I walking in my truth?" And when that becomes your new normal—when self-worth no longer hangs on your reflection, but flows from your recognition—you become unstoppable. Not perfect. Not flawless. But fully, finally, free.

You will know you've won the war when silence in front of the mirror no longer feels like judgment—but peace. When you no longer rush to fix, to tweak, to compare—but to listen. Because beneath the skin, beneath the expression, there's a story being told. A story of every time you stood back up. Every time you cried and still showed up. Every time you felt fear and did it anyway. That's what the mirror holds now—not flaws, but evidence. Proof that you lived, that you tried, that you endured. And that kind of reflection? That's not something you need to change. That's something you need to honor.

Some mornings, you will still forget. You'll wake up and feel the old tug—of not being enough, of needing to do more, be more, change more. But now, you'll have a different voice inside you. One that doesn't shout, but reminds. It says, "You've been here before. And you know the truth now." And the truth is this: confidence isn't built in the mirror. It's built in the moments when you refuse to betray yourself. When you walk out of the house without needing approval. When you choose to rest instead of hustle. When you tell someone the truth, even if it makes you less likable. Those are the real victories. Invisible. Internal. But revolutionary.

Because self-worth was never about what they see—it was about what you believe. The mirror was only ever a witness. It never had power. You gave it power. And now, you're taking it back.

Not to destroy the mirror, but to redefine it.

To turn it from battlefield to blessing.

To look at your reflection, scars and all, and say: "You are not my enemy. You are my evidence. My echo. My becoming."

And in that moment, something shifts—not just in you, but in the world around you. Because once a person no longer fears their own re

And so, you stand before the mirror one last time, not as a warrior, but as a witness. No more fighting, no more fixing, no more flinching. You stand tall in your own skin, not because the world finally approves, but because you do. At that moment, the glass doesn't hold any more power over you. It's just a reflection—of light, of angles, of truth, of time. And you see yourself for what you've always been: a human being, complex and imperfect, but whole. Whole in your struggle. Whole in your growth. Whole in your right to be.

The mirror no longer demands answers, because it has already seen the only one that matters: you.

And in this stillness, there is a quiet, profound peace. You understand now that the battlefield was never the reflection in the glass. The battlefield was always inside you. And winning this war wasn't about changing who you were. It was about realizing you were enough from the very start.

You've already won.

VIII

The Masks We Wear

There comes a moment in everyone's life where you stop recognizing the person in the mirror. Not because your face has changed, but because the person staring back isn't you anymore. It's a version you built — brick by brick — to survive. To be accepted. To be praised. To be safe. Somewhere along the line, you stopped living as you and started living as the idea of who you thought you were supposed to be. That's the mask. And the scariest part? You've worn it for so long, you forgot what your own skin feels like underneath.

We don't start out this way. As kids, we are loud and honest and wild. We cry when we're hurt. We laugh when we're happy. We ask too many questions. We're curious and chaotic and messy and magical. But the world doesn't want to be wild. It wants to be manageable. It wants to be polite. So piece by piece, it begins the quiet work of taming us. "Sit still." "Don't say that." "Act like a good boy." "Smile even if you're sad." And we learn — painfully early — that being real has consequences. So we adjust. We start to wear what's acceptable. Not clothes. Masks.

Some of them look confident. Some look like politeness. Some even look like success. But they all share one thing in common: they hide who we really are. And we wear them not out of pride — but fear. Fear of being too much. Fear of being not enough. Fear of being rejected for the things we feel too deeply. So we silence our truth to be liked, to be praised, to be seen as "put together." But the great irony is, the more we try to be seen, the less of us actually are.

I wore my first real mask in school. It wasn't anything physical. It was the way I stopped asking questions. The way I pretended I understood things I didn't. The way I started caring more about what others thought than what I truly felt. I got good at it. So good, in fact, that I didn't even notice I was pretending anymore. I was the "well-behaved" one. The "disciplined" one. The "confident" one. People admired that mask. And for a while, I did too — because it kept me safe. But masks don't protect you. They imprison you.

And here's the part no one tells you: the mask doesn't just fool others. It fools you. You forget how to cry. You forget how to feel. You even forget how to want — because everything you've done for years wasn't for you, it was for the image you were trying to protect. And somewhere in that performance, the real you starts whispering: "Is this it?" But that whisper gets drowned by applause. People clapping for your mask while your soul stays silent.

The most dangerous thing isn't being disliked. It's being loved for something you're not. Because that love traps you. You think, if I take this mask off, will they still love me? So you don't. You keep smiling. Keep achieving. Keep pretending. And the applause gets louder. But inside, you're screaming. Because the person they love isn't you — it's your performance.

We wear different masks for different rooms. One for the family. One for friends. One for the world. Some people wear the mask of the joker — always funny, always "fine" — while silently breaking inside. Others wear the mask of the achiever — always driven, always successful — while carrying the weight of crippling self-doubt. And then there are the quiet ones — the ones who say little, feel much, and hide everything. These are the most dangerous masks, because they look like nothing at all.

But make no mistake: every mask is heavy. And eventually, it breaks you. Not all at once. Slowly. Secretly. You start feeling tired even after sleeping. You start avoiding mirrors. You start feeling like a stranger inside your own body. That's not burnout. That's not laziness. That's the cost of being inauthentic. It's your soul begging for oxygen. And the only way to breathe again — is to take it off.

But taking off the mask isn't easy. It means being seen. Fully. Unfiltered. It means saying, I'm not okay — and risking that someone might walk away. It means admitting that you're human — with fears and doubts and wounds you haven't healed yet. But it also means finally, finally, being real. And once you taste that kind of freedom, the fake stuff becomes unbearable.

There's a strange moment that happens when the mask slips — not when you take it off on purpose, but when life rips it from your face. A heartbreak. A failure. A breakdown. A death. Suddenly, you're too exhausted to perform. You stop smiling. You stop pretending. And the people around you look confused. "What's wrong with you?" they ask, not realizing they've only ever met the costume — never the person beneath. And in that silence, you learn who truly loves you... and who only loved the character you played.

I remember the first time I tried to be completely real in front of someone. My voice shook. My hands trembled. Every part of me screamed to retreat — to go back to the safe version, the acceptable version. I almost did. But something told me: No one can love you if you keep hiding. So I said the truth anyway. And they didn't run. They didn't flinch. They just stayed. And that moment taught me something I'd never forget — real love only finds you when you stop pretending.

But not everyone stays. Some people will leave when they see the real you. That's the price of honesty. And it hurts. Deeply. But that pain is holy. It's the proof that you're finally living without disguise. Every soul that walks away from your truth makes space for one that can embrace it. You start to realize: it's not about how many people accept you. It's about whether you accept yourself without the mask.

You start building a new relationship — not with the world, but with the stranger in the mirror. The one you abandoned to please everyone else. You ask yourself questions you never had the courage to before: What do I really want? What am I really feeling?

Who am I when no one is watching? And the answers don't come all at once. Sometimes they arrive in tears. Sometimes in anger. Sometimes in long silences where the only thing you can feel is your own heartbeat. But they come.

And slowly, something beautiful begins to happen: you begin to feel alive. Not just existing. Not just functioning. But alive in the rawest, messiest, most vibrant way possible. You start laughing and it feels real. You start crying and it feels clean. You no longer shrink yourself to fit into someone else's comfort zone. You don't laugh at jokes that hurt you. You don't say "yes" when your body screams "no." You no longer live in survival mode. You live in truth.

The world doesn't make this easy. It still rewards the polished. The perfect. It Was palatable. But you begin to care less. Not out of arrogance, but clarity. Because when you've lived for years behind a mask, authenticity becomes sacred. You begin to value deep over popularity. Real over pretty. Peace over praise. You start choosing friends who see you, not just admire you. You start walking away from spaces that force you to perform. You start honoring your inner voice — the one you ignored for far too long.

And most of all, you start forgiving yourself — for all the years you pretended. Because those masks weren't worn out of malice. They were worn out of need. You did what you had to do to survive a world that told you to dim your light. But now... now you're choosing to live. Fully. Loudly. Honestly.

The truth about masks is this: they never fully protect us. They only hide us from the real risks — the ones that could set us free. We live in a world obsessed with perfection, with image, with what's polished and proper. And in this world, authenticity feels like a luxury we can't afford. It feels dangerous. It feels vulnerable. Because we've been taught that if we show the parts of us that are messy, unpolished, or broken, we'll be judged. Rejected. Dismissed. So, we keep the mask on — the mask of strength, of happiness, of having it all together. And we think that's the only way to survive.

But the truth is, the more we hide behind that mask, the more we suffocate. We begin to lose sight of who we truly are, until one day we can't even remember the last time we were genuinely happy. The laughter we've been sharing isn't real. The conversations aren't authentic. We've been playing a part for so long that we've forgotten how to just be.

I've worn the mask of the overachiever for years. In school, in work, in relationships — always trying to be the best. Always trying to prove myself. Always trying to earn my worth in the eyes of others. But there came a time when I realized that no matter how many awards I won, no matter how many goals I crushed, there was always something missing. Something deep inside me that felt empty. It was the realization that I was living for someone else's approval. For someone else's idea of success.

I had become a master at wearing the mask of the "successful" person. But behind the mask was a man who was terrified. Terrified of failure. Terrified of not measuring up. Terrified of being exposed. And all of that fear drove me further into performance mode — until the day I couldn't breathe anymore. I reached a breaking point. The mask started cracking. It wasn't just exhaustion. It was something deeper. It was the realization that I couldn't keep pretending I was okay. I couldn't keep pretending I had it all together. I was falling apart. And I was terrified that if I let anyone see it, they would see me as weak. As a failure.

But when I finally allowed myself to fall apart, when I took off the mask for the first time in years, something incredible happened. The world didn't collapse. People didn't leave me. In fact, some of them embraced me more deeply than ever before. They didn't want the perfect version of me. They wanted the real me. The flawed, broken, scared, yet deeply human version of me. And in that moment, I understood something that changed everything: the people who truly care about you will never love you for the mask you wear. They love you for the soul beneath it.

We've all heard the phrase "be yourself," but what does that really mean? How do you be yourself when the world rewards everything but who you truly are? How do you strip off the layers of masks you've built over the years? It starts with being honest with yourself — not just about your strengths, but about your flaws, your fears, your regrets. And when you accept those parts of yourself, something magical happens. You stop seeing them as weaknesses. You stop seeing them as things to hide. You start seeing them as pieces of your story. Pieces that make you real. And when you start embracing those pieces, you begin to embrace your own power.

The thing about masks is they only work if you believe them. If you believe the lie that you're not enough without them. But when you wake up to the truth — when you see the mask for what it is — you realize that it never had the power you thought it did. And when you take it off, the world doesn't fall apart. It becomes clearer. You can breathe again.

I remember the first time I took off the mask of "having it all together." It was in a room full of people I'd known for years. I'd always been the "strong one" in the group — the one who had the answers, the one who could handle anything. But that day, I was tired. Tired of pretending. Tired of holding everything together. I said it, and I said it out loud: I'm not okay right now. It was the first time in years I allowed myself to say those words. And the response was not what I expected. People didn't pity me. They didn't judge me. Instead, they surrounded me. They listened. They shared their own stories of struggle. And in that moment, I realized something: we are all carrying masks, and it's only when we shed them that we can truly connect.

The vulnerability you feel when you remove the mask is terrifying. It's raw. It's messy. But it's also where the magic happens. It's where you find your true self, unafraid to be seen. And when you're no longer hiding behind a facade, you become free. Free to be imperfect. Free to be loud when you're hurting, quiet when you need space. Free to be you — unapologetically.

This journey isn't easy. In fact, it's one of the hardest things you'll ever do. But it's worth it. Because when you take off the mask, you stop living for validation. You stop living for applause. You stop living to meet other people's expectations. And you start living for yourself. For your truth. For your fire.

So, take a deep breath. Look in the mirror and ask yourself: Who am I, really? And then let the mask slip. Let it fall away. Because underneath all the layers of performance, there is something beautiful waiting to be revealed — you.

When we begin to unmask ourselves, it feels like standing on the edge of a cliff, knowing that the only way forward is to jump. The idea of freedom is intoxicating, but the fear of what we'll find beneath the surface keeps us tethered to the familiar. What if I'm not enough without the mask? What if the world rejects me once it sees the real me?

But the truth is, we have always been enough. We were born enough. The mask we wear — the one that hides our vulnerability, our flaws, our fears — is the lie we tell ourselves in order to survive in a world that punishes authenticity. But that mask doesn't shield us from the world. It only keeps us from connecting to it. It keeps us isolated, hollow, pretending to be someone we're not.

I remember walking through a season of profound loneliness — not because I didn't have people around me, but because I wasn't truly seen. I had perfected the art of blending in, of playing the role that people expected of me. And for a while, it felt safe. But deep inside, I was aching. I was yearning for connection, not the kind that comes from performing, but the kind that comes from being. The kind of connection that says, "I see you, even in your brokenness. I see you, and I love you anyway."

The problem with wearing a mask for so long is that it becomes your identity. You forget who you are underneath it. And when you forget who you are, you forget your power. You forget that you are enough — just as you are. We all are. It's only when you shed the mask that you begin to realize your true potential.

But the shedding is painful. It's messy. It's a process. There are moments when you'll feel naked, exposed, and vulnerable. The world may not always be kind to those who take off their masks. You may face rejection, judgment, and the harshness of a society that values perfection over authenticity. But here's the thing: every rejection you face is just a sign that you are shedding the parts of you that no longer serve you. The people who can't handle your truth weren't meant to be in your life anyway. There's freedom in vulnerability. When you take off the mask, you open yourself up to the possibility of true connection. You allow people to see you for who you really are. And in doing so, you invite them to be real with you as well. The greatest relationships are not built on masks, but on raw honesty. They are built on the understanding that we are all flawed, we are all struggling, and we are all worthy of love, just as we are.

One of the most profound moments of clarity came to me when I stopped pretending to be perfect. I was at a point in my life where everything felt like it was falling apart. My career was in shambles. My personal life was a mess. And for the first time in years, I didn't know what to do. I felt lost. But in that space of uncertainty, I realized something. I didn't need to have it all figured out. I didn't need to pretend anymore. I could be vulnerable. I could be honest. And I could let people see the parts of me that were broken, because those broken parts were the ones that made me whole.

When I let go of the need to be perfect, the weight lifted. I stopped pretending. I started showing up as I was, messy, unpolished, but real. And that's when things started to shift. People began to respond to me differently. They stopped seeing the mask and started seeing me. The raw, unfiltered version of myself. And that version of me was met with acceptance, with love, with respect — not because I had it all together, but because I was willing to be vulnerable. I was willing to be human.

And in that moment, I understood the true power of vulnerability. It's not about being weak. It's about being real. It's about showing up without the facade, without the armor, and allowing yourself to be seen, flaws and all. Because when you let go of the mask, you give others permission to do the same. And in that shared space of honesty, something beautiful happens. You form connections that are deep, meaningful, and rooted in truth.

The masks we wear are not just barriers between us and others. They are barriers between us and ourselves. When we wear a mask, we are telling ourselves that we are not enough as we are. But when we take the mask off, we begin to embrace our true selves — all of our beauty, all of our mess, all of our imperfection. And in that act of embracing ourselves, we unlock a power that no mask could ever give us.

It's time to let go of the mask. It's time to stop pretending to be someone we're not. It's time to show up in this world as our true, authentic selves. And in doing so, we will find that the world, instead of rejecting us, will embrace us — exactly as we are. Because real magic doesn't happen when we perform for others. The magic happens when we allow ourselves to simply be.

As I stand here today, I realize that the most powerful thing we can do is to show up, fully and completely, as ourselves. No more hiding behind the masks. No more pretending to be something we're not. Because the truth is, the world doesn't need more perfect people. It doesn't need more polished, flawless images. What the world needs — what we need — is realness. Raw, unfiltered, unapologetic realness.

I used to think that by hiding my flaws, by covering up my weaknesses, I could protect myself from the harshness of the world. I thought that by wearing the mask of confidence, strength, and success, I could avoid rejection. I thought I could avoid failure. But in the process, I lost sight of what it truly means to be alive. I lost sight of the power of being vulnerable. The power of showing up as you are — not because you're perfect, but because you're human. And there is something infinitely beautiful in that.

The moment you take off the mask, you step into a new realm of possibility. You become free from the chains of expectation. You give yourself permission to be messy, to be real, to be flawed. And in that freedom, you start to experience life in a way you never thought possible. You no longer live for the approval of others. You no longer chase after perfection. Instead, you live for yourself — for your truth, for your authenticity. And when you do that, the world begins to respond differently.

The people around you will either accept you or not. And that's okay. The people who accept you for who you truly are, the ones who embrace you without judgment, will become your tribe. They will become the ones who walk with you on this journey of growth, self-discovery, and healing. And the ones who can't handle your authenticity? They will fade into the background, and that's okay too. Because the people who matter will always see the real you. And that's all that matters.

Taking off the mask doesn't mean we stop striving. It doesn't mean we stop growing. It doesn't mean we stop aiming for greatness. It simply means that we do it from a place of truth. We do it because it's what we want, not because it's what others expect. We do it because we are worthy — just as we are — and we no longer need to hide behind a facade to prove it.

It's time to embrace the power of vulnerability. It's time to embrace the power of being real. Because when you stop hiding behind the mask, you step into your own power. You stop letting fear control you. You stop letting the opinions of others dictate your worth. You stop letting society's expectations shape your identity. And when you do that, you become unstoppable.

There's a profound strength in being vulnerable. It's not a weakness. It's not fragility. It's raw, untapped power. The kind of power that comes from embracing yourself fully — flaws, scars, and all. When you stop pretending to be perfect, you unlock a strength that no mask could ever give you. And that strength is what will carry you through the toughest of times.

I want you to take a moment and ask yourself: What masks am I wearing? What parts of me am I hiding in order to fit in, to gain approval, or to avoid judgment? And then ask yourself: What would happen if I took off those masks? What would happen if I allowed myself to be truly seen — not just the polished, perfect version of me, but the real, raw, messy version? What would happen if I stopped pretending?

I'll tell you what will happen: you will discover a new level of freedom. You will step into your own power. You will finally realize that you are enough — not because of the mask you wear, but because of who you are at your core. And when you embrace that truth, when you allow yourself to be fully you, the world will open up in ways you never imagined.

The masks we wear may seem safe at first, but they only trap us in a prison of our own making. The moment we take them off is the moment we reclaim our freedom. The moment we stop pretending is the moment we start living — truly living. So, take off your mask. Let yourself be seen. Let yourself be heard. Let yourself be real. Because that's where the magic happens. That's where the transformation begins. And that's where you will find the true power that has been inside you all along.

IX

The Fire You Forgot You Had

There's a moment in every life when the fire inside you burns so bright, it feels like you could conquer anything. It's the spark of ambition, the passion that drives you, the unstoppable force that makes you feel invincible. But somewhere along the way, we lose it. We become consumed by the noise of the world — expectations, failures, doubts — and the fire starts to flicker. We convince ourselves that it's gone, that it was just a spark, something that was never meant to last.

But here's the truth: the fire never left. It was never extinguished. It was just buried beneath the weight of life. And it's time for you to rediscover it.

Remember those days when you were untouchable? When your dreams felt like they were just within reach, and you believed you could achieve anything? That fire wasn't just a feeling. It was your power — your inner drive, your purpose, the essence of who you are. Somewhere along the way, you forgot about it. You let fear, criticism, and the pressure to conform dim that light. But I'm here to remind you: that fire is still within you. It's waiting to be reignited.

I'll tell you something — the Phoenix is a powerful symbol of rebirth. A creature that rises from the ashes, born again from the destruction of its former self. It's a beautiful metaphor, one that represents the possibility of transformation, of starting over, of becoming something greater than before. But here's the thing about the Phoenix: it's fictional. It's a story, a myth passed down for generations, meant to inspire us but never really within our grasp.

But what if I told you that the true rebirth is not a myth at all? What if I told you that the real fire inside of you — the one that you think has burned out — is the same thing that makes you unshakable, just like a creature in the wild? Enter the Honey Badger. A creature much smaller and much less graceful than a Phoenix, but one that has something far more powerful: the refusal to back down. This little animal is known to face off with lions, snakes, and even larger predators, showing an incredible fearlessness and sheer willpower. It doesn't care how big the threat is. It doesn't care how many obstacles stand in its way. The Honey Badger simply keeps going.The Phoenix may rise from the ashes, but the Honey Badger never stops fighting. It doesn't need a dramatic rebirth. It simply continues to push forward, facing challenge after challenge, with no thought of quitting. It fights for its survival with unwavering determination. And that's the fire you forgot you had.

I remember a time when I, too, felt like the Phoenix — as if I was burned out, as if the fire within me had been extinguished by failure, by doubt, by the pressure of the world. I couldn't see my way forward. But the more I looked inward, the more I realized something: I wasn't a Phoenix, I was a Honey Badger. The real fire isn't in mythical stories or dramatic transformations. It's a daily fight. It's in the refusal to let life break you. It's showing up again and again, even when the odds seem impossible. The fire is in your ability to keep going, to keep believing, to keep fighting — not because you're invincible, but because you are resilient.

Just like the Honey Badger, you don't need to rise from the ashes to prove your strength. Your power is in the persistence, the grit, and the resilience to face whatever challenges come your way. You don't need to wait for the perfect moment or the grand transformation. Your fire has always been within you — and all you need to do is rekindle it with the same fierceness the Honey Badger shows every single day.

The hardest part is taking the first step. When you've been living without that fire for so long, it's hard to even imagine what it would feel like to have it back. You've become so accustomed to the darkness that the light seems foreign. But here's what I want you to understand: you don't have to wait for the perfect moment. You don't have to wait for life to align perfectly, or for everything to fall into place. You just have to take the first step.

Reignite that fire with small actions. Do the things that make you feel alive again. Start with something simple — something that makes your heart race with excitement, something that reminds you of the power you hold within you. It might be a goal you've forgotten about, a passion you've buried deep inside, or a dream you've been too afraid to chase. Whatever it is, take that first step. It doesn't have to be grand. It just has to be real.

Once you take that first step, you'll begin to feel the fire inside you stir. It won't be instantaneous, but it will start to come back. Slowly at first, but then with more intensity. And soon, you'll feel the familiar warmth, the familiar drive, the familiar hunger to go after what you want.

The fire you thought was lost is not gone. It's still there, waiting to be kindled. You just have to stop pretending it's not. You have to stop letting fear and doubt smother it. You have to stop telling yourself you're not worthy of greatness, that you're not capable of achieving your dreams. The fire inside you is proof that you are. The fact that you can feel that spark, even in the darkest of times, means that it's still there. It's waiting for you to unleash it.

When you tap into that fire, you tap into the truest version of yourself. You reconnect with the part of you that believes in possibilities, that sees opportunity even in adversity, that knows nothing is impossible. You remember that you are not defined by your failures or your setbacks. You are defined by your ability to rise again, by your willingness to keep going when it feels like the world is against you. The fire inside you is the fuel that will drive you to rise higher, to push through the pain, to continue when everyone else would give up.

And when you find that fire again, you'll realize that the world was never as cold as you thought. The fire is not just a source of warmth for you — it's a light for others as well. When you rediscover your passion, your purpose, your drive, you begin to inspire others to do the same. You become a beacon of possibility. You show them that no matter how lost they feel, no matter how dim their own light may seem, the fire is still there. It's waiting to be reignited.

So, don't give up on your fire. Don't let the world tell you it's gone. It's still there, deep within you, burning brighter than you think. All you have to do is remember it.

I want you to think about the Phoenix for a moment. It's one of the most powerful metaphors used to symbolize transformation — a magnificent creature that rises from its ashes, reborn and stronger than before. A story of resilience and triumph. We've all heard the myth: the Phoenix burns, only to emerge renewed and unstoppable, a symbol of what's possible after destruction. It's a beautiful story, one that gives us hope in moments of despair, reminding us that we can always start over, no matter the failure or pain we've endured.

But here's the thing about the Phoenix: it's a myth. A fictional story that captures our imagination, but it's not real. No matter how much we wish for it, we can't wait for the heavens to make us into something new after we've been burned. We don't get to rise from the ashes in a flash of fire and glory. The true power lies not in a mythical rebirth, but in the reality of our everyday fight.

Now let me tell you about the Honey Badger. Much smaller, much less graceful, and certainly not a creature of myth, the Honey Badger is a true force of nature. If you've ever watched footage of one, you'll see something incredible: this tiny creature faces down lions, cobras, and other predators with a relentless attitude. It doesn't care about its size, the threats, or the danger. It simply keeps going. No matter what stands in its way, it charges forward with a ferocity that defies logic. The Honey Badger doesn't wait for a mythical rebirth. It doesn't need to rise from ashes. It just keeps fighting, keeps moving forward with the certainty that no challenge is too great for it to handle.

That's the real lesson we need to learn. The fire inside you isn't about waiting for some grand, mythical transformation. It's about realizing that the real power is in showing up every single day, even when it feels impossible. The Honey Badger doesn't need to wait for a perfect moment. It simply does what it needs to do, regardless of the odds. And that's where your fire lies — not in a grand moment of transformation, but in the everyday fight, in the constant effort to keep moving, keep pushing, keep believing.

The fire you thought was lost isn't gone. It's just been buried under the weight of your doubts, your setbacks, your failures. But if you take a moment and look within, you'll find it. And once you recognize that fire, you won't need a mythical Phoenix to inspire you. You'll find that you are the Honey Badger, and that's all you need to face any challenge that comes your way.

The Phoenix is an alluring symbol. In our minds, it represents something grand — a dramatic rise, a miraculous transformation. We envision the moment when everything falls apart, and then, somehow, from the very ashes of destruction, we emerge reborn, renewed, stronger than before. The myth itself speaks to our deepest desires: the idea that no matter how far we fall, there's always a chance to rise again, more powerful than ever.

But as much as we love this story, we need to face the truth: the Phoenix is a fantasy. It's a story, a dream we cling to in times of failure, a comforting thought that tells us that we'll be granted a grand rebirth. But rebirth doesn't come in an instant, and it doesn't come with the convenience of waiting for life to hand us a fresh start. Life is too unpredictable for that. The Phoenix's flames are beautiful in theory, but they don't exist in the real world. The truth? Transformation isn't an overnight process. It's the slow, messy, difficult work that happens every day, in the trenches.

That's where the Honey Badger comes in. It's real, it's gritty, and it's unapologetically relentless. This small, fierce creature doesn't wait for a miraculous transformation. It doesn't seek perfection. When the Honey Badger faces its enemies — from lions to venomous snakes — it doesn't back down. It doesn't have wings to soar or magic to transform. Instead, it has unbreakable determination and the will to fight, no matter the odds.

The Honey Badger doesn't need a second chance; it makes its own. It doesn't worry about what happened yesterday or what might happen tomorrow. It's only focused on right now, on surviving, on pushing forward, and on continuing the fight. And that's the true power. The Honey Badger is an embodiment of a fire that's never extinguished, a fire that's stoked by sheer persistence, and a refusal to give up.

This is the fire inside you. It's the fire you forgot you had, buried deep beneath the weight of doubt, failure, and the fear of what might come next. When life knocks you down, it's not the dramatic rebirth of a Phoenix that you need. It's the fierce, stubborn determination of a Honey Badger. It's the ability to get back up, over and over, without needing to be "reborn" or "transformed." The fire inside you isn't waiting for some mythical moment of perfection. It's in every choice you make to continue, to keep pushing, to refuse to let go of your dreams. It's not about how many times you've failed or fallen; it's about how many times you've risen, how many times you've chosen to keep fighting.

Think about it: When you've been knocked down, what's the first thing that happens? You might feel overwhelmed, defeated, even ashamed. You may wonder if the fire has truly gone out. But I promise you — it's still there. It's buried under all that doubt, under the weight of your fears and disappointments. And the moment you choose to fight, to push through that discomfort, to rise once again, that fire will light up. The flame will flicker, then grow stronger, until it becomes the raging force it was always meant to be.

The real test isn't in waiting for a perfect moment of transformation. It's in the moments when everything feels like it's falling apart, when you feel like there's nothing left to give. That's when you need to remember that you are the Honey Badger. You don't need permission to rise. You don't need a grand cosmic sign. You just need to keep going. Even when everything around you tells you to stop, even when the world seems to be collapsing — you keep going.

Because here's the truth: the fire that makes you keep fighting, even when you're exhausted, even when you're ready to give up, that's the fire that's been within you all along. It's not the Phoenix's grand rebirth. It's the daily courage to stand up, fight back, and keep moving forward. And that, my friend, is the most powerful fire of all. So, when you feel like you're losing your way, when you think that the fire inside you has burned out, remember this: you are not a Phoenix waiting to rise. You are a Honey Badger with an unbreakable spirit, and that fire will never go out as long as you choose to keep fighting. We weren't born without it. As kids, we ran wild with curiosity, hunger, and courage. We didn't care about looking foolish. We spoke our minds. We tried, failed, and tried again without shame. We had dreams that were loud, messy, and unapologetically bold. That was the fire — raw, untamed, and completely ours.

The world began handing us masks — quiet ones at first. Be good. Don't make mistakes. Don't stand out too much. Don't speak unless you're sure. Fit in. Be realistic. Those words didn't sound like commands, but over time, they chipped away at our flame. Every time we hesitated instead of speaking, every time we stayed small to make others comfortable, a bit of the fire dimmed. Until one day, we looked in the mirror and didn't recognize who we had become. Not because we changed — but because we forgot who we were.

We started believing that we weren't meant for greatness. That passion was for other people. That confidence was reserved for the "naturally gifted." We buried the fire under responsibility, under fear, under other people's expectations. And slowly, the voice inside us that once screamed, "I was born for more" began to whisper — until even the whisper went silent.

The world won't come with a lighter and reignite your flame. That's your job. Every risk you take, every truth you speak, every time you step into discomfort — you're throwing kindling on that fire. Every time you say no to fear and yes to your purpose — even with shaking hands — you're reminding yourself, "I still have it. I never lost it. I was just too afraid to look for it." You don't need a rebirth. You need a reunion — with your wild, fearless self.

The one who wasn't afraid to dream. The one who didn't shrink. The one who knew that fire wasn't something to find — it was something to unleash. And remember — you don't need to burn the world down in one day. Sometimes, all it takes is a single spark — a hard conversation, an honest journal entry, a moment of courage when everything in you says to quit. The fire you forgot you had doesn't need to roar. It just needs to be believed in again.

So how do you find that fire again? You don't — because it was never lost. You buried it. You hid it behind fear, behind routine, behind trying to be who the world said you should be. And now, if you want it back, you don't wait for it to magically appear — you build it, with trembling hands and an unwilling heart. The fire doesn't return in comfort; it returns in chaos, in discomfort, in doing the one thing your body resists but your soul craves. That conversation you're afraid to have? That's where it lives. The truth you're swallowing? That's where it's hiding. That decision you keep postponing because you don't feel ready? That's where the flame waits. You don't get the fire back by reading about it. You get it by bleeding for it. Every time you choose courage over comfort, every time you lean into pain instead of numbing it, every time you speak instead of staying silent — you're not just remembering who you are, you're reclaiming who you were before the world told you to forget. We think fire is a feeling. It's not. It's not motivation or hype. It's a decision. It's a daily, ruthless practice. You think confidence comes before action, but it's the other way around — you act while scared, and confidence follows like a shadow that finally realizes you're not waiting anymore. Stop sitting in the dark waiting for a matchstick of inspiration. You are the damn match. You don't need healing to start. You don't need clarity to move. You need movement to find clarity. You need pain to remember your edge. And yes, it will burn. But you weren't built for safety. You were built to feel the heat of your own potential and still walk forward. That fire isn't something you lost — it's something you abandoned. So now, go back. Kick down the door. Stand in the flames if you must. Because what comes out of that fire isn't ashes — it's you, unmasked, unafraid, and finally on fire.

Have you ever noticed how we romanticize the phoenix — a bird that bursts into flames and rises from the ashes, majestic, glowing, divine? We cling to that image like it's our comeback story, like fire is something we wait to be consumed by and reborn from. But let me break that illusion: the phoenix isn't real. It's a myth — beautiful, but distant. You know what's real? The honey badger. Tiny. Fierce. Unbothered. Outnumbered. But completely, relentlessly unapologetic about its fire. It doesn't wait to be reborn — it fights back while still bleeding. It charges lions. It raids venomous snake nests. It doesn't wait for permission or applause — it just exists in full volume, with zero concern for how the world sees it. And that? That's real fire. Not some poetic rise from mythical ashes, but dirty, clawing, gritty defiance in the face of everything designed to break you. You don't need to be reborn. You don't need to turn into something new. You need to remember what you already are — before you started shrinking, before you traded your teeth for politeness and your claws for comfort. The fire you forgot you had isn't about becoming majestic — it's about becoming undeniable. It's not about rising from ashes, it's about refusing to burn in the first place. And the moment you stop waiting to feel worthy and start showing up like the damn honey badger — bold, raw, and unbothered — is the moment the world starts realizing they can't tame you anymore. You were never made to be mythical. You were made to be real, relentless, and on fire — always.

Let's stop pretending. You didn't lose your fire. You abandoned it. Piece by piece, choice by choice. Every time you said, "I'll do it later." Every time you stay silent to avoid judgment. Every time you let your talent rot in exchange for approval. You let fear sit in the driver's seat and you called it humility. You let comfort suffocate you and name it peace. And now you wonder why you feel numb. Why don't your eyes burn with hunger anymore? Why do your days feel quiet even when everything around you is loud. It's because you traded your fire for a cage. A cage made of expectations, fake smiles, overthinking, and silent suffering. And the worst part? You got good at pretending. Good at looking "fine." Good at blending in. But here's the truth: deep down, you're furious. Furious at the version of you that backed down. That stopped fighting. I chose the easy way because it was safe. That ignored every gut instinct begging you to wake up. And that fury? That's the spark. Don't ignore it. Don't numb it. Don't silence it. That's your fire kicking, screaming, clawing to be remembered. So feel it. Feed it. Let it burn every version of you that played small. Stop waiting for life to push you. Start punching back. Not tomorrow. Now. While your knees still shake. While your voice still cracks. While fear still whispers. Because real fire doesn't wait for perfect timing. It erupts the moment you decide you're done being forgettable.

You keep telling yourself you're waiting for a sign, for clarity, for a perfect moment where everything lines up and you suddenly become who you were meant to be. But here's the real reason you haven't moved — you're scared of who you could become. Scared of how powerful, loud, raw, and relentless you'd have to be if you actually said yes to your fire. Because let's be honest — it's easier to keep pretending you're "figuring things out" than to own the fact that you've been hiding. Easier to binge content than to create. Easier to complain than confront. Easier to call it burnout than admit you've been living a life that doesn't even belong to you. And if that hurts to hear, good. Let it. Because the version of you that lives on fire isn't polite. It doesn't care about being understood or accepted. It doesn't wait for approval. It disrupts. It breaks patterns. It walks into rooms like it belongs there — even when no one invited it in. You weren't born to be half-alive. You weren't designed to live quietly. The fire in you was meant to take up space, to change things, to rattle cages — especially your own. But that will never happen if you keep apologizing for your intensity, your ambition, your hunger. Stop shrinking. Stop negotiating with fear. Stop editing yourself to be digestible for a world that was never built to handle your full heat. You weren't made to fit. You were made to burn.

Now that the fire's awake — what do you do with it?

You use it. You weaponize it. You turn it into motion. Because fire that stays inside too long? It starts burning you from the inside out. So you move. Not in giant leaps. Not in dramatic exits. But in non-negotiable, ruthless, daily action. You get up earlier than you want. You go harder than you feel. You say no to comfort like it's a poison — because it is. You stop just talking about discipline and actually bleed for it. You don't need a 5-year plan. You need a 5-second decision. The moment your alarm rings — get up. No thinking. No snoozing. No bargaining. The moment you hesitate to speak your truth — speak it anyway. The moment you feel fear — lean in. Move toward it. Because every time you choose motion over mental noise, your fire gets louder. You stop being a prisoner of your thoughts and start becoming the kind of person who does, not just dreams. And you don't need motivation — you need momentum. You need to stop waiting to feel ready and start training your body to move regardless. You want that inner fire to stay? You feed it through discipline, through decisions, through discomfort. You make yourself impossible to ignore — not to the world, but to yourself. Every single day, you build a fire so strong, even your worst moments can't put it out.

Here's the real shift: you don't just build the fire — you become it. You stop identifying as someone who's "trying to get better" and start owning that you're already dangerous. Already worthy. Already built for more. That shift doesn't come from affirmation quotes or soft podcasts, it comes from war. From the daily, quiet, brutal war with your weaker self. And the people who win? They don't wait for discipline to feel good. They don't ask themselves if they're in the mood. They wake up and go to war with comfort like it killed someone they love. Because it did. It killed the version of them they could've been. And that's the difference — most people mourn their dreams like it's some sad story. But the ones who rise? They get furious. Furious at wasted time. Furious at hiding. Furious at the fake smile they've worn for years. And they don't just use that rage — they become that fire. So now, ask yourself: are you still playing victim to your moods, your past, your fear? Or are you ready to rise like someone who doesn't need to be saved anymore? Because at some point, you stop looking for fire in books, people, places... and you realize — it was always you. The difference between the lost and the legendary isn't talent. It's this: they didn't wait to feel like fire — they decided to live like it.

If you've read this far, it's because some part of you is still alive. Still burning. Still hungry. But here's the question that'll split your life into before and after: what are you going to do about it? Not tomorrow. Not when life calms down. Right now. You've been given a spark. A reminder. A punch to the guy that says: You were never average. You just acted like it for too long. You don't need more time. You don't need more signs. You don't need permission. You need to get uncomfortable, get angry, and get moving. Get rid of the lie that says you're not enough. Destroy the version of you that flinches. That waits. That whispers instead of roars. This is your moment. To reclaim what you buried. To stop being agreeable when your soul is begging for war. To stop editing your fire so it fits into small spaces and small conversations. Let it all go. The fake calm. The fake plans. The fake identity. You were born to disrupt, to challenge, to lead, to bleed, to become the walking reminder that fire doesn't ask to be seen — it demands it. So stand up. Right now. Say it out loud. "I am fired. I am not waiting. I am not hiding. I am not done." Burn the old version of you. Light the match. Step into the smoke. And never look back.

X

FLY ANYWAY

You can build a rocket ship and still be told you're too young to fly it. You can climb the mountain, only to be told you took the wrong route. You can pour your soul into preparing for a job interview, only to be dismissed because you don't have "enough experience." This is the world we live in—a world where dreams are often measured by outdated templates, where passion is filtered through the lenses of practicality, and where even brilliance is sometimes rejected because it doesn't look like the norm. But I'm telling you this: fly anyway.

Even in 2025, parents across the country still sell their lands, pawn their jewellery, give up their heritage—just so their children can sit in a classroom. They melt their lives into the fire of hope. And that fire is passed down into the hands of their children—not as a burden, but as a torch. They send their sons and daughters to college, believing that education is the key that will unlock every door. But what happens when the child, despite passing every test, is told they're still not enough? "No experience." "Not qualified." "Lacks soft skills." That's the moment the dream cracks. That's the moment the fire stutters.

But here's the truth that no one wants to say out loud: the format doesn't work anymore. The one-size-fits-all path is broken. What worked yesterday might destroy you today. And yet, we follow it—blindly, loyally—because we were told it's the "safe" way. I don't blame the parents. How could I? They loved us the only way they knew how. They followed what they believed was right. But the flaw isn't in their love—it's in the system that made love a transaction: give education, get success. But life doesn't work like that. Life doesn't guarantee returns.

You want the truth? The only thing that works—truly works—is skill. Not a skill someone forced into you. But a skill you carved out of your own soul. The kind of skill that stands strong even when the storm hits. The kind that lights up when you're alone, jobless, and on the edge of giving up. The kind of skill that says, "No matter where I am, I can create. I can solve it. I can build. I can lead." And you only build that skill through discomfort. Through pain. Through choosing the road no one's walking on.

When I was young, I used to think confidence meant loudness. Now I know it's a quiet fire. I know it's what you build in silence, not in applause. You may hear all these stories, metaphors, quotes—but don't mistake them for perfection. I'm not fully confident in myself. I have my flaws, my failures, my broken mirrors. But you know what makes me different? I don't run from them. I wear them like medals. I've failed exams, broken down, questioned myself—but every time, I stood back up. Just like iron, the more heat you give it, the more you can shape it. People are the same. You don't need someone to save you. You need to burn a little. You need to bleed for your own dreams.

I used to dream of being a film director. It sounded funny to some, silly to others. I was good at storytelling. In school, I used to write stories in English class and score top marks for them. My teacher would praise me in front of the whole class. But one of my friends laughed when I said I wanted to be a director. "This isn't like writing a story in your grammar class," he said. "Directing is expensive. It takes years." And maybe he was right. But I was passionate. I didn't care how long it took.

That's when I found something amazing: Kamal Haasan, the legendary Tamil actor, once wrote the script for Devar Magan in just seven days. Imagine that. A film that went on to win five National Film Awards, considered a landmark in Indian cinema—written under pressure, not over years, but in a week. Why? Because he wasn't just working. He was driven. Passion is the only fuel that lets you race against time. Kamal Haasan described it as a "pleasure-filled, almost childish game." That's what passion does—it turns pressure into play. And if he can do it, why can't we? You see, talent matters. But desire—desire is the real beast. You can teach skills. But you can't teach hunger.

People often ask me about my name—Celestin Ignatius Raj. "Why does your name sound so feminine?" "Why is it so hard to pronounce?" Growing up in North India, my name was always mispronounced. I hated it. I came home from school angry, asking my mother why she gave me such a name. She told me it was named after the birth of Jesus—Celeste, from Latin, meaning heavenly. But that didn't stop the ridicule. That didn't stop the confusion.

Then one day, my dad sat me down and changed everything. He told me, "Your name is a bottle. You have to fill it. Fill it with your courage, your passion, your work. Make it so powerful that one day, people who used to mock it now pause in respect when they hear it." That stuck with me. My name wasn't just a word—it was a mission. I wasn't born into a brand. I was born to build one. My name carries legacy—my father's name, my family's values. And now, it carries purpose. That's what I want for everyone reading this: make your name matter. Not by shouting it. But by showing up for it. Every single day.

Be the kind of person whose consistency is louder than their promises. Whose journey speaks louder than their claims. Let your name become a synonym for strength, for effort, for integrity. Let it become a story in itself. Every time you show up despite fear, every time you choose growth over comfort, every time you act with courage when no one is watching—you build your name because those who fly anyway are the ones who are remembered—not for where they landed, but for daring to take off when the sky said no.

You know what hurts the most? Not the rejection itself—but the silence that follows. When you've worked for years, stayed up nights, sacrificed friendships, missed birthdays, gave up sleep, gave up peace—just to end up in a waiting room with no answer. When you refresh your inbox ten times in an hour, hoping the job application gets through. When someone less qualified gets the seat you deserved—not because you weren't good enough, but because someone else had connections, fluency, or just looked the part. That silence isn't empty—it's loud. Loud with questions. Loud with self-doubt.

But in that silence, you have a choice: breakdown... or break through.

That's what most people never tell you. That every single person who ever became somebody started out as nobody with a fire. Behind every achievement, there's an invisible war. The sleepless nights. The crippling anxiety. The years of being ignored. The mental breakdowns that come after giving your best and still falling short. But here's the thing—resilience is not a gift. It's a habit. You don't wake up strong. You decide to be strong. And you decide it every damn day.

I remember one evening after school, I walked home with tears in my eyes. Some seniors laughed at my name again. "Celeste? Is that a girl's name?" I didn't even answer. I was tired of explaining. Tired of defending. I came home, slammed the door, and shouted at my mom: "Why me? Why did you give me this name?" And she, like always, calmly said, "It's a beautiful name, son. A heavenly name. Named on the birth of Jesus. You'll understand one day." But I wasn't ready for that calmness. I needed anger. I needed revenge. What I didn't realize then, was that my revenge would not be words. My revenge would be my success.

And then came my father—quiet, direct, unwavering. He looked me in the eye and said, "Celestin Ignatius Raj. Sounds strong, right?" I hesitated. He continued, "It will sound strong... when you become strong. A name means nothing if the person behind it is weak. But if you carry it with fire, people will remember it even after you're gone." That one sentence hit me harder than any insult I ever received. He turned my shame into a mission.

Let me tell you this: if you're ashamed of something you were born with—your name, your skin, your accent, your roots—then you haven't looked deep enough into your purpose. You haven't started long enough into your fire. You're not supposed to fit in. You're supposed to stand out. You're supposed to carry the weight of difference and turn it into strength.

And if they tell you it's impossible, show them the story of Kamal Haasan. A man who wrote Devar Magan—a script that went on to win five National Film Awards—in just seven days. A script born not out of luxury or freedom, but out of pressure. And yet, he called it a "pleasure-filled, almost childish game." That's the mindset of greatness. Passion so intense that even deadlines become playgrounds. That's what happens when you love what you do so much that even pain becomes art.

You know what's funny? People will tell you it takes years to master something. But passion doesn't check the clock. Kamal Haasan didn't write greatness in seven days. He delivered it in seven days. But it took a lifetime of pain, experience, and obsession to reach that moment. So when people say, "It's too late," or "You need more time," tell them this: it's never about time. It's about intensity.

Some of you reading this feel broken right now. Jobless. Hopeless. You feel like the world moved forward and left you behind. You applied for everything and heard back from nothing. You tried your best and failed anyway. And now, you're scared. Scared that maybe you're not good enough. But I want you to hear me loud and clear: you're not broken. You're just beginning.

You don't have to look successful to be worthy. You don't need a company to approve your value. You are the company. You are the product. You are the CEO of your own mission. And guess what? You're underpriced. The world just doesn't know your worth yet. That's okay. That's how all revolutions begin—quietly, invisibly, underestimated. Let them underestimate you. Let them mispronounce your name. Let them mock your dreams. Then let them watch you rise. Because those who fly anyway don't wait for permission. They don't wait for perfect weather. They don't wait for applause. They just fly—with broken wings, with tired hearts, with borrowed courage. And somehow, they soar.

But let's talk about those falls. The ones you don't expect. The ones that come out of nowhere and hit harder than you ever thought possible. They say it's easy to rise when you're at the top, but the real test is how you stand up when you're at the bottom. When the ground seems like it's all you'll ever know. And it's in those moments, those brutal, raw, tear-filled moments, that you realize: there's no one coming to pick you up. There's no one to save you. Except you.

This is the part of the story that no one tells you. They don't tell you that the path to success is riddled with scars—both visible and invisible. They don't tell you that you'll burn out. You'll doubt yourself. You'll question whether all the pain, all the sacrifice, was worth it. It's easy to talk about success when you're looking at the finish line. But what about the journey? What about those long, empty stretches where no one applauds, no one cheers, and the world seems to forget you're even trying?

There was a time in my life when I almost gave up. No one knew, not even my closest friends. I was struggling with a dream that seemed just out of reach. I was doing everything I could—working harder, staying later, giving everything. But for months, it felt like I was running on a treadmill. My progress was invisible, the results were slow, and the setbacks were loud. I felt like I was screaming into a void, waiting for some kind of sign, some kind of breakthrough.

And then, it hit me—there is no breakthrough without the breakdown. There is no rise without the fall. It's not about how hard you work or how much you sacrifice—it's about your ability to endure when everything falls apart. It's about getting back up when you don't want to. It's about moving forward when every single part of you says, "Just stop." Because here's the hard truth: if you can't survive the falls, you'll never earn the flight.

I think of the story of the phoenix. A bird that's consumed by fire, reduced to ashes, only to rise again—stronger than before. But here's what they don't tell you about the phoenix. It doesn't rise by chance. It rises by choice. Every time it's burned, it chooses to rise. It chooses to build its wings, again and again, even when it's certain the world is just going to burn it down again. That's resilience. That's passion. That's the kind of fire you need to carry inside you if you're ever going to fly.

The world may tell you it's impossible. The world may tell you to wait for the perfect moment, for the perfect opportunity. But when has the perfect moment ever existed? When has anyone ever waited for everything to line up before they went after their dreams? It doesn't work like that. You can wait forever, and you'll still never feel ready. You know why? Because you were never meant to wait. You were meant to do it. You were meant to start—before the conditions were perfect, before you had all the answers. Start now. Build your wings in the process.

And if you fall? Fall with dignity. Fall with strength. Let every fall remind you of how high you've risen before. Let it be a reminder that, with every failure, you're one step closer to your breakthrough. The more you fall, the more you learn. The more you fail, the more you grow. And the more you grow, the harder it will be for the world to ignore you.

I've seen it in my own life. Every setback, every loss, every time I thought it was over, turned out to be just the beginning of something greater. The strength I thought I lacked was hidden inside me all along, waiting to be discovered in the hardest of times. It was never about how talented I was or how much luck I had—it was about how much I was willing to endure.

Look at the stories of those who changed the world—people like Steve Jobs, Elon Musk, Oprah Winfrey. Do you think they woke up one day with everything figured out? No. They had failures. They had doubts. But they kept going. They kept moving forward, one step at a time, even when no one believed in them. Even when they didn't believe in themselves.

There's a quote that says, "It's not about how many times you fall—it's about how many times you get up." I've always believed this. Because every time you fall, the world is watching—not just to see if you'll get back up, but to see if you'll get back up stronger. And that's the key to everything. The strength is in the comeback. The real victory is in the fight, the refusal to stay down, the decision to stand up every single time you fall.

So, here's the challenge for you: fly anyway. When the world tells you it's too hard, when the dream seems impossible, when the odds are stacked against you—fly anyway. Because your wings were never meant to be delicate. They were forged in fire, built in pain, and destined to soar.

When you look around, you'll see people who are caught in the trap of waiting. Waiting for the right time, waiting for permission, waiting for someone to tell them they're ready. But here's a secret that not many people are brave enough to admit: you'll never feel ready. There will never be a moment when the stars align, when you have all the answers, when the fear is completely gone. That's the illusion. The truth is, you will always have doubt, and you will always face uncertainty. The difference between those who soar and those who stay grounded is not the absence of fear, but the courage to move forward despite it.

Think about the moment you first tried to ride a bike. You were scared, right? Your hands shook, and you had no idea whether you'd fall or stay upright. But you kept going. And each time you fell, you learned. You adjusted. You made small tweaks to your balance, your stance, your mindset. And eventually, you got better. Riding a bike became second nature, and the fear that once held you back became a distant memory. The same thing happens when you chase your dreams. The first steps are always the hardest. The fear of failure is loud, but if you ignore it long enough, it fades into the background, and your passion becomes the loudest voice in your head.

I remember when I first decided to start my business. I had no idea what I was doing. I was scared out of my mind. I didn't have the resources, the experience, or the support that I thought I needed. All

I had was a burning desire to make it work. It was like trying to ride a bike for the first time in a storm. The winds were strong, and the rain kept hitting me in the face. But I kept pedaling. Slowly at first, but steadily. I made mistakes, I fell, I faced countless obstacles, but each time, I got back up. I adjusted my approach, I learned from my failures, and I moved forward. And eventually, just like learning to ride a bike, it became easier.

You see, the moment you choose to step into the unknown, to step into discomfort, that's when the magic happens. That's when you grow. If you never make the choice to face the fear, to fight through the doubt, you'll stay exactly where you are. But if you're willing to keep moving forward, even when everything inside you is screaming to stop, you will evolve. You'll learn to transform your fear into fuel, your setbacks into stepping stones. The fear that once tried to hold you back will be the same energy that propels you forward.

I've met so many people in my life who have incredible dreams but never take the first step. They talk about what they want to do, but when it comes time to take action, they freeze. They worry about the consequences of failure, the opinions of others, or their own perceived inadequacies. But I've also met people who take that leap, even when they don't have everything figured out. And do you know what happens to them? They succeed. Not because they were smarter, not because they had better resources, but because they acted. They made a decision to step into uncertainty and push forward with everything they had.

There's a lesson in this: if you want to change your life, change your mindset about failure. Stop viewing it as something to avoid and start seeing it as a tool for growth. Every failure is a lesson in disguise. Every setback is a redirection to something better. Every no is one step closer to a yes. The key is to keep moving. Keep moving, no matter how slow. Keep moving, no matter how many times you fall. Because each step forward, no matter how small, gets you closer to the life you want to live.

And remember, you don't need a big stage to make a difference. You don't need millions of people watching you or applauding you to feel successful. The most powerful impact comes from the small moments—the moments when you choose to act, even when no one is watching. When you show up every day, even when the world seems indifferent. When you do the work, even when the results aren't immediate. That's where true greatness is built.

Look at the people who have changed the world. The ones who have made a real difference. They didn't wait for the perfect time. They didn't wait for someone to give them permission. They stepped up and took ownership of their dreams. And yes, they failed. Yes, they struggled. Yes, there were moments when they thought about quitting. But they kept going. And that's the difference.

In the end, it's not about the destination. It's not about reaching some grand achievement that everyone can see. It's about the person you become along the way. The resilience you develop, the strength you build, the courage you cultivate to push through when everything else tells you to give up. It's about looking back at the person you were and realizing how far you've come. It's about knowing that, despite the failures, the struggles, and the doubts, you kept going. You chose to fly.

So, here's my challenge for you: the next time you feel fear, don't run from it. Fly anyway. The next time you doubt yourself, don't retreat into the shadows. Fly anyway. The next time life knocks you down, don't stay there. Fly anyway. Because your wings were built for this. And with every step you take, with every challenge you face, you are becoming the person you were always meant to be.

In life, it's not the absence of challenges that defines us, but the way we respond to them. The difference between those who soar and those who stay grounded isn't luck or circumstance; it's the will to keep going, even when the road is rocky, the winds are strong, and the destination feels far out of reach. Every time you choose to move forward despite the fear, despite the obstacles, you are strengthening your wings. You are sharpening your resilience. And with every challenge you face, you are one step closer to becoming the person you were meant to be.

But let's take a moment to acknowledge that we don't rise to greatness because we never fall. We rise because we choose to get back up each time we do. There's a famous quote by Nelson Mandela that says, "I never lose. I either win or learn." Think about that for a second. If we treat our failures as lessons instead of losses, then we begin to see them as stepping stones toward our growth. If we approach every failure with this mindset, every setback becomes an opportunity to rise, evolve, and come back stronger.

This mindset isn't easy to adopt. It's not something that comes naturally to most of us. We are wired to protect ourselves from pain, from disappointment, from failure. But the truth is, it's through those very experiences that we build character. It's through the struggle that we discover our strength. We become resilient not because we've never faced adversity, but because we've faced it head-on and emerged on the other side more capable, more confident, and more determined than ever.

Take the story of J.K. Rowling, for example. Before she became the household name behind the Harry Potter series, Rowling faced rejection after rejection. In fact, her manuscript was turned down by twelve different publishers before someone finally saw the potential in her work. Think about that. If she had given up after the first rejection, after the third, or after the tenth, the world would never have known Harry Potter. But she kept going. She kept writing, kept believing in her story, and eventually, her perseverance paid off. Today, her name is synonymous with success, but it wasn't always that way.

Rowling's story isn't unique. There are countless examples of people who have faced failure after failure, only to rise to the top because they didn't give up. Michael Jordan, widely regarded as one of the greatest basketball players of all time, was famously cut from his high school basketball team. He could have given up then, but he didn't. He used that rejection as fuel to work harder, to improve, and to prove everyone wrong. That determination eventually led him to become a six-time NBA champion and a global icon.

But it's not just famous figures who experience failure. Every one of us has faced setbacks, whether it's in our careers, relationships, or personal goals. The difference is how we choose to respond. Do we let our failures define us? Do we allow our doubts to dictate our actions? Or do we take those failures, learn from them, and use them as stepping stones to our next success?

Here's where the power of consistency comes in. Success is rarely the result of a single great moment. It's the culmination of small, consistent actions over time. It's the daily choices we make that determine our outcomes. You don't need to make a massive leap every day. What matters is that you keep moving forward, even when it's tough. Even when it feels like you're not making progress. It's the steady, consistent effort that builds momentum. The small wins that lead to big victories.

Think about the story of the bamboo tree. The bamboo tree spends the first five years of its life underground, barely visible, but during that time, it's building an incredibly strong root system. Then, in the sixth year, it shoots up rapidly, growing up to 80 feet in just a few months. The tree's strength comes from the consistent growth and foundation built in the dark, unseen years. And that's how success works. The early years may seem slow. Progress might be hard to see. But all the while, you're building a foundation that will support the growth to come.

Sometimes, it may feel like nothing is happening. Like all your efforts are in vain. But just like the bamboo tree, your work is building a foundation, laying the groundwork for something bigger than you can see right now. And when the time is right, you'll soar—just like that bamboo, shooting up toward the sky.

The key to breaking through that invisible barrier is persistence. Keep showing up. Keep doing the work. Keep believing in yourself, even when no one else does. You won't always see immediate results, but that doesn't mean you're not making progress. Keep your eyes on the bigger picture, and trust that the work you're putting in today is shaping the person you'll be tomorrow.

As you move forward on your own journey, remember this: you don't have to have it all figured out. You don't need all the answers right now. What you need is the courage to begin. The strength to continue. And the faith to know that every step you take is a step toward the life you were meant to live.

So, fly anyway. Even when you're not sure of the path. Even when the world tells you it's impossible. Even when the doubt creeps in and tells you to stop. Fly anyway. Because your wings are meant to soar, and the world is waiting for you to show up and make your mark.

Every challenge you face is an opportunity for transformation. It's easy to get discouraged when things don't go as planned, especially when the world seems to be moving faster than you are. But the truth is, growth doesn't always happen in visible, dramatic ways. Often, it's the small, incremental changes that have the biggest impact on our journey. Every time you push through a challenge, every time you choose to take that next step despite the odds, you are rewriting your story. You are becoming the person you were always meant to be.

There's a powerful metaphor that illustrates this perfectly—the process of shaping steel. Steel, when it's first forged, is a soft, malleable material. It has to go through extreme heat, intense pressure, and a series of refining steps to become the strong, durable substance we know. That transformation, that metamorphosis, doesn't happen overnight. It takes time, patience, and an immense amount of force. But when the process is complete, the steel is unbreakable.

Just like steel, you are being forged through life's challenges. The heat of failure, the pressure of setbacks, and the refining of your character make you stronger. With every obstacle you face, you're becoming more resilient. Every difficulty you encounter adds a layer of strength, making you capable of handling even bigger challenges down the road.

But here's the catch: just because you're going through difficulty doesn't mean you're not moving forward. It's easy to think that because things aren't going perfectly, you're not making progress. But success isn't about perfection. It's about perseverance. It's about showing up every single day, doing your best, and trusting that each step forward is getting you closer to where you need to be.

One of the most important lessons I've learned on this journey is that nothing worth having comes without a fight. It's not enough to simply wish for success or dream about the future. You have to work for it. You have to commit to it with every fiber of your being. That means being willing to face rejection. It means being willing to sacrifice. It means doing the work even when it feels like nobody's watching.

This doesn't mean you should be blind to the obstacles in front of you. On the contrary, recognizing the challenges you're facing is essential to overcoming them. But what matters is how you respond. Do you let the challenges stop you, or do you rise above them? Do you let failure define you, or do you redefine what failure means?

Think about the story of Thomas Edison, the inventor of the lightbulb. He faced countless failures in his quest to invent a reliable, affordable light source. In fact, when he was trying to create the filament for the lightbulb, he failed thousands of times. But instead of seeing those failures as defeats, he viewed them as lessons. He famously said, "I have not failed. I've just found 10,000 ways that won't work." Edison's persistence eventually paid off, and his invention changed the world. His ability to embrace failure, learn from it, and continue working toward his goal made all the difference.

You don't need to be a genius to succeed. You just need to have the determination to keep going, no matter how many times you fall. That's the secret to success—to fail, to get back up, and to keep moving forward with renewed strength and resolve. Your failures are not signs that you should stop. They are the signs that you are growing, that you are evolving, and that you are becoming more equipped to handle the challenges ahead.

In the end, success is not just about what you achieve. It's about who you become in the process. It's about developing the kind of character that stands tall in the face of adversity. It's about cultivating resilience, persistence, and courage—qualities that will carry you through the toughest times and help you emerge stronger than ever.

And here's the most important part: you don't have to do it alone. Surround yourself with people who support you, who believe in you, and who push you to be better. Whether it's friends, family, mentors, or colleagues, having a strong support system can make all the difference when things get tough. Don't be afraid to lean on others, to ask for help, or to share your struggles. You don't have to carry the weight of the world on your own. There is strength in community, in knowing that others are rooting for you and willing to help you rise when you fall.

The journey to success is never a straight line. It's filled with twists, turns, and bumps along the way. But if you stay true to your purpose, keep moving forward, and never stop believing in yourself, you will get there. And when you do, you'll look back at all the obstacles you faced, all the moments of doubt and failure, and realize that they were the very things that made your success possible.

So, fly anyway. Even when the winds are against you. Even when the skies are stormy. Even when the world tells you it's impossible. Keep flying. Because you were born to soar.

I once heard someone say, "Don't clip your wings just because others are afraid of heights." That hit me like a lightning bolt. Most people don't fear failure—they fear judgment. They fear being seen trying and falling. They fear being laughed at for dreaming too loud or flying too high. So they choose safety. They choose silence. They choose to walk when their heart is made to soar. But here's the truth—they're not laughing because they're right. They're laughing because they stopped flying a long time ago.

The system we grew up in, especially in a country like India, often teaches us to obey more than to create. To memorize rather than to question. To follow rather than to fly. We are told to take the safest route—the one with the most job security, the one with the fewest risks. And yet, we glorify the stories of the rebels and risk-takers. We quote Kalam, admire Dhirubhai Ambani, celebrate Ratan Tata—but we punish their spirit when it shows up in our own classrooms or homes. That contradiction is dangerous. It creates a culture where dreams are framed and hung, but never lived.

But let me tell you—dreams are not meant to be framed. They are meant to be built. With bricks of effort, cemented with consistency, and painted with your own shade of madness.

Let's talk about a truth many are scared to face: most people are not living their dreams, not because they failed, but because they never started. They spent too much time calculating risks, waiting for the perfect moment, listening to people who never built anything on their own. What if Kamal Haasan waited? What if he decided that seven days wasn't enough? What if he feared the critics, the comparisons, the weight of writing for Sivaji Ganesan? We wouldn't have Devar Magan. We wouldn't have a masterpiece born under pressure. Some of the greatest creations in history were born not because conditions were perfect, but because the creator decided to create anyway.

Your story will never be perfect. The timing will never be right. Your resources might always feel too little. Your skills might still be forming. But if the fire is real—if the purpose is honest—start anyway. Fly anyway. Because the world is waiting for that one soul who refuses to settle. That one person who decides, "Even if the world is asleep on me, I'm wide awake on my purpose."

You don't owe anyone an explanation for your passion. You don't need permission to chase something that sets your heart on fire. And no, you don't need a committee of approvals to tell you that you're ready. Readiness isn't something given—it's something declared. You declare you're ready when you show up in the rain, when you work in silence, when you train in the dark—because you know your moment in the light will come. And when it does, you'll be too focused on building your legacy to care who once doubted your wings.

This is what I want you to remember: every time you choose action over excuses, you're rewriting the narrative. Every time you chase passion instead of perfection, you're becoming unstoppable. There will always be people who don't understand. Let them misunderstand you. There will always be people who leave. Let them go. The people meant to fly with you will meet you at your altitude.

If you ever feel like you're the only one chasing something nobody else understands, good. That's what vision feels like in the beginning—lonely. But it's not loneliness you're feeling. It's elevation. It's altitude sickness. Not everyone can breathe where you're headed. The higher you fly, the fewer people you'll see around you—but the clearer your view becomes. This clarity? It's not a curse. It's your compass.

Think of the eagles—they don't flap endlessly like pigeons. They wait. They rise when the wind gets violent. Because the very storm that terrifies others is what lifts them higher. That's your story too. You were not born to be caged in opinions, trapped in systems, or measured by outdated checklists. You were born for impact. And that impact starts the moment you stop trying to be understood—and start trying to be effective.

Let the world keep asking, "Who do you think you are?" And let your work whisper back, I'm becoming who I was born to be.

And when you reach that point—where rejection doesn't shake you, failure doesn't define you, and silence doesn't stop you—you will have finally stepped into your real name. Not the one they gave you at birth. But the one your actions earned. The one your character carved. The one your heart fought for.

Because in the end, we all get remembered for two things—how deeply we lived and how boldly we loved. That's your legacy. Not your degree, not your followers, not your resume. It's who you became when life tried to shrink you. And you chose to expand anyway.

This is your permission to be unreasonable. To believe anyway. To try anyway. To fail loudly and rise louder. To speak when your voice shakes. To build when your hands tremble. To walk when the road disappears. This is your license to live unapologetically—without waiting, without shrinking, and without asking anyone's permission to matter.

Fly anyway. And never come back down.

So here we are, at the end of the pages, but not the end of your path. If you've made it this far, know this: you are not ordinary. You never were. The world might've tried to label you, reduce you, silence you, but you were born without permission — and that, in itself, is your permission to rewrite the rules.

You don't need a stamp of approval to be great. You don't need a podium to lead. You don't need perfect conditions to begin. You need belief. You need fire. You need that stubborn whisper inside you that says, "Even if the world says no—I'll go anyway."

Because the truth is, no one is coming to save you. Not a teacher. Not a recruiter. Not society. And that's not something to fear—it's something to celebrate. Because you've always had everything you needed inside you. The courage. The pain. The purpose. The fight.

Don't just live. Set fire to your life. Don't just work. Create. Don't just follow. Lead. And when it gets hard—and it will—remember that you are not here by accident. You're here to build something that lasts beyond you.

So speak your truth, even if your voice shakes.

Love with everything, even when it hurts.

Create, even when no one understands.

Fall—but fall forward.

And when they ask you how you did it, how you survived, how you stood tall in storms meant to break you.

Smile and say, *"I was born without permission. And I flew anyway."*

AFTERWORD

If you've made it to this page, thank you—for staying, for feeling, and for daring to believe. Writing Born Without Permission was not about proving anything. It was about uncovering what was always there but buried: strength, clarity, and the fire to live honestly. My hope is that this book reminds you that your voice matters, your dreams matter, and your story deserves to be lived loudly.

The world may not always applaud difference, but history remembers those who refused to be erased.

Go create. Go fail. Go rise.

Go live without permission.

— Celestin Ignatius Raj

Bibilography

Books & Writings

Bandura, A. (1997). Self-efficacy: The exercise of control. W.H. Freeman and Company.

Brown, B. (2010). The power of vulnerability [TED Talk]. TEDxHouston.

Coelho, P. (1993). The alchemist (A. Clarke, Trans.). HarperOne.

Clear, J. (2018). Atomic habits: An easy & proven way to build good habits & break bad ones. Avery.

Dweck, C. S. (2006). Mindset: The new psychology of success. Random House.

Frankl, V. E. (2006). Man's search for meaning (I. Lasch, Trans.). Beacon Press. (Original work published 1946)

Gladwell, M. (2013). David and Goliath: Underdogs, misfits, and the art of battling giants. Little, Brown and Company.

Haasan, K. (1992). Devar Magan [Film script and interviews]. Retrieved from archived interviews and regional publications.

Peterson, J. B. (2018). 12 rules for life: An antidote to chaos. Random House Canada.

Pope, G. U. (Trans.). (1886). The Sacred Kural or the Tamil Veda of Tiruvalluvar. Oxford University Press.

Sharma, R. (1997). The monk who sold his Ferrari: A spiritual fable about fulfilling your dreams and reaching your destiny. HarperSanFrancisco.

Sinek, S. (2009). Start with why: How great leaders inspire everyone to take action. Portfolio.

Thomas, E. (2012–present). Motivational speeches and sermons. Retrieved from www.etinspires.com

Historical and Conceptual References

The Shark Experiment. (n.d.). Referenced in behavioral psychology and motivational training modules.

Wootz Steel (Urukku). (n.d.). Historical Indian metallurgy. Sources include archaeological studies and cultural heritage records.

The Bumblebee Flight Myth. (n.d.). Popular motivational metaphor referenced in aviation and personal development literature.

Upanishadic and Indian Philosophical References. (Various dates). Concepts of Dharma, Karma, and Swadharma.

Original Frameworks and Insights

Raj, C. I. (2025). The Ignatius Theory of Internal Fire. Personal philosophy introduced in Born Without Permission.

www.ingramcontent.com/pod-product-compliance
Lightning Source LLC
Chambersburg PA
CBHW020611160726
47991CB00002BA/731